THAT
IMMORTAL
SEA

CLIFFORD BAX

THAT IMMORTAL SEA

A MEDITATION UPON THE FUTURE OF RELIGION AND OF SEXUAL MORALITY

" Hence in a season of calm weather
Though inland far we be,
Our souls have sight of that immortal sea
Which brought us hither . . ."

19 33

LOVAT DICKSON LIMITED
38 BEDFORD STREET LONDON

LOVAT DICKSON LIMITED, 38 BEDFORD STREET,
LONDON, W.C.2, *and at* ST. MARTIN'S HOUSE,
BOND STREET, TORONTO

First Printed 1933
Second Impression 1933

Printed in Great Britain by R. Clay & Sons, Limited, Bungay, Suffolk.

To PAUL ARUNDEL NORTH

My Dear Paul,

You will probably find, now that you have received the book of which I spoke to you, that it differs considerably from the book which you expected. I hope that it will not disappoint you. I hope, too, that in associating it with your name I am not presenting you with an unusually large White Elephant, for there is no doubt that a dedication can become an embarrassment.

Perhaps you expected me to give a nutshell account of various religions, to attack one and extol another, to use the impressive language of a metaphysical text-book, or to build round my ideas a stout rampart of quotations from acknowledged authorities: and all that I have done, as you will now find, is to present very simply a point of view about what we might call, for the sake of brevity, " sex " and " the soul." Long ago I doted upon an argument as ardently as upon a game of chess, but as time has passed I have come to believe that logic without " feeling " is like a car that has a brake but no engine. I wanted, therefore, only to suggest why a modern man may think of himself as a spiritual being who will outlast death, and why promiscuity is not likely to be the solution which our century will find for the problems of sexual behaviour. Argument between friends may be fruitful, but a book goes out from the author's room to the publisher, from him to the book-shops and the professional critics, and from them, if they are well-disposed, to the " general reader." An author, therefore, is always at the disadvantage of not knowing who may turn over his pages. People have various reasons for " not believing in the soul "; some because they believe only what the scientists tell them, others because their upbringing has implanted within them certain bitter and obstinate prejudices: and it is obviously impossible to argue with a thousand or even with a hundred persons. That, then, is why, instead of arguing, I have merely stated a point of view, but, at the risk of seeming presumptuous, I will add that I believe it to be a point of view which is coming toward us, as it were, from the near future.

The problems of sexual conduct we have, manifestly, to solve while we are alive, for we may assume that they will be of no interest to us when we are disembodied. The problem of the soul's permanence is one to which all of us must inevitably know the true answer some day; but our management of life depends so greatly upon our conception of what death means that few of us can altogether put the question aside. I, presumably, shall learn the answer a long time before my step-son learns it. Well, I can only assure you of my conviction that when I am far away from this world, while you are still grappling with its tasks and puzzles, I shall have realised that the ideas which you will find in the earlier part of this book are a very dim adumbration of the amazing truth.

CLIFFORD BAX.

December 1932.

CONTENTS

PART I

I

IF a man of twenty-five, like another Rip van Winkle, had fallen asleep in 1900 and had waked up again in 1930, he would find himself in so changed a world that for a long time he would not be able to get his bearings. Everyone can realise how astonished he would be by the material changes of the last thirty years. Cocktails, gramophones and negro dances would considerably surprise him. He would be amazed by our tube-railways, by the absence of horses in the streets, by the myriads of motor-vehicles that sped and snorted past him, by the aeroplanes over his head and by the Arabian Nights miracle of a radio-set. Even now he would not be sixty years old. Many thousands of living people, therefore, have watched the world change before their eyes, but, not having fallen asleep in 1900, they adjusted themselves to one invention after another, and for this reason accept the new world with as little astonishment as do their juniors.

It is not at all easy, however, to realise how

bewildered our Rip van Winkle would be by the change in the mental outlook of the average man or woman. In particular, he would not be able to understand for some weeks our attitude toward the two deepest interests of humanity—toward religion and sex. He would find out, for instance, that, compared with his world of thirty years ago, very few people go to church. He would be surprised to discover that even his cook and housemaid prefer to spend their Sundays elsewhere. Before long, indeed, he would learn that most people, not only in England, but also in every civilised country, are living without any religion and do not believe in the existence either of God or of the soul. Furthermore, he would be continually scandalised by what he would regard as our extreme laxity in the matter of sex. If we remember that women in the days of his youth were supposed to have no sexual needs or desires, and that he hardly ever saw anything of a girl's figure, unless he visited a Parisian music-hall, we shall understand the embarrassment with which he would attend a typical revue or even turn the pages of an illustrated weekly. Above all, he would certainly be conscious that the mental atmosphere of our age is very much more restless than the atmosphere in which he passed his youth.

The world of that period will not come back.

People will never again think as the Victorians thought about either sex or religion. Indeed, there are many persons, especially among our intellectual leaders, who suppose that religion is now for ever a thing of the past. Some of them, in fact, assume that the thoroughgoing materialism of present-day Russia merely foreshadows the future philosophy of the whole world. The aim of this book is to suggest that, for all their ability, they are wrong; that the Russian attitude, far from becoming universal, will not endure even in Russia; and that the men and women of the near future are likely to recover, though not in the old form, a belief that there is a God in the universe and an immortal spirit in a man.

This, I am well aware, is a bold project; but I do at least realise that we are far away from the time when a man could present himself as a teacher, expecting that other men would listen reverently while he told them how they should behave or what they should believe—far away even from the confident era when Ruskin (rivalling Mr. Barrett in Rudolf Besier's admirable play) could roundly assert that " God does not approve " of this or of that. I have no " messianic delusion," no fantastic notion that my book is capable of converting the world to the point of view which it sets forth. On the contrary, I shall be fortunate if I can keep a single companion to the end of this journey. Some readers will abandon me because they will abhor my forecast of what is going to happen in respect of sex-morality; others because I shall not be overawed by traditional religion; others again—a much larger number —because, writing in a scientific age, I shall not be overawed even by science.

Merely to have used already the words " God," " immortality " and " the soul " is to have alienated a certain type of reader, a type which perhaps we may term the university-minded. We have all known examples of this type—persons who cannot take a book seriously unless it is written in the sesquipedalian jargon of professional metaphysics. Thought is to them only an elaborate game, played by professors, in which no human emotions are at stake. In their company we cannot safely observe even that toast is delicious. Any two persons of the normal kind would agree or disagree on the spot; but the university-minded man, engaged in his fantastic game with the others, would require us to state when, where and to whom toast can accurately be said to be delicious; precisely at what tempera-ture a piece of scorched bread can truly be called toast; and whether deliciousness lies in apprehension, experience or retrospect.

All this may be entertaining to those for whom thinking is only a pastime, or a battle of wits, but most men realise that we never get anywhere unless we think in shorthand. A conversation, for example, will progress at a snail's pace if the partners in it are merely trying to trip each other up. It can be fruitful only if they co-operate; and I shall be using old and familiar words because I am writing for those who are in search of a few ideas to which they may hold fast in the intellectual and moral confusion of our time; to whom philosophical speculation is of interest only in so far as it may modify a man's feeling about life and death; and who, in consequence, will accept these old words as having much the same significance for him and for me.

The average man does not now believe in God or the soul. I think that he has no need to abandon a belief in either, and that his children, when they have grown up, will construct a religion and a morality for themselves. The bold—and perhaps presumptuous —purpose of this book is to suggest the probable basis of the religion and morality which will ultimately characterise the twentieth century. And both, undoubtedly, will be simple.

II

IF we could go back a hundred years, or even sixty, we should find ourselves intellectually among strangers. In spite of Gibbon, Voltaire and the sceptical tone of the eighteenth century, at least before John Wesley transformed it, most men of a hundred years ago had a simple and definite religion and morality. To-day, for example, I received a catalogue of second-hand books, and as I was turning the pages my attention was caught by Item 279. This was an autograph, a " two-page letter, signed with initials," from William Wordsworth to one of his sons. The letter bears no date, but it may have been written about 1830; and here is the fragment of it which the bookseller used as a bait for purchasers:—

" From the black seal of this letter you will have concluded that your poor Aunt Wordsworth was no more. It is not so. Dear Aunt Sarah has gone before her. She never gained strength after the severe fever was subdued. On Thursday she sank alarmingly; at noon yesterday we had not the slightest hope of her recovery; and it pleased God that she should depart this life before the day was closed. She was an excellent woman, and we trust that she is among the blessed."

To most of us the sentiment in these lines will seem as faded as the ink with which they were written. A modern man may well be surprised that a great poet should have supposed that God had, as it were, personally decided to withdraw Aunt Sarah from this world, or have conceived that after her death she had been instantly transported into the society of "the blessed." Even his use of black sealing-wax, in token of mourning, removes the writer to a great distance from ourselves. And yet in the course of the nineteenth century fifty thousand Aunt Sarahs must have died, and fifty thousand persons who were not great poets must have sent their tidings in almost identical language.

If, again, we turn to Nelson's diary and read the page that he wrote when the French and Spanish fleets were actually in sight off Cape Trafalgar, we shall get the same feeling that an immense difference of outlook divides us from the men of 1805. "At daylight," wrote Nelson, " saw the enemy's combined fleet from east to E.S.E.; bore away; made the signal for order of sailing; and to prepare for battle; the enemy with their heads to the Southward; at seven the enemy wearing in succession. May the Great God, whom I worship, grant to my country, and for the benefit of Europe in general, a great and glorious victory. . . . To Him I resign myself and the just Cause which is entrusted to me to defend."

We may smile at the poet's implication that Aunt Sarah would not so soon have joined the blessèd unless God had been pleased that she should, and at the admiral's assumption that God would be looking on at the Battle of Trafalgar and probably deciding that England should win it; but we may also envy the simplicity of mind with which these two great men, and a huge majority of their contemporaries, took for granted that all human affairs, from a naval battle to Aunt Sarah's fever, were watched and directed by a benevolent Deity. The men of those times had their own troubles, but they also based their lives upon an almost childlike view of the world which is now as far away from us and as irrecoverable as the slow-moving life and the unspoiled countryside of a hundred years ago.

Indeed, as I am writing these words, on a Sunday evening, the bell of a London church is monotonously summoning all good Christians to attend " divine worship," and it has to my ear a mediæval sound. I know that the typical man of our time, or even the typical woman, will not respond to it. He or she will be hurrying to "the pictures," or returning at great speed from a motor-car dash into the country, or settling down to an evening of bridge or with the wireless. I know that they do not believe that God takes a hand in the business of mankind, and that they would say, with a poet writing in 1908,

> "The good ship Immortality
> Has gone down, like the sun."

They live in a state of mind so different from that of Nelson and Wordsworth that, spiritually, they are hardly of the same species.

Again, a small incident caused me, a few months ago, to realise vividly how much the world has altered in its view of sexual behaviour. Coming away from a rehearsal, I waited for an omnibus at one of the official stopping-places in Regent Street. About half a dozen persons had already assembled there, and within a few seconds we were joined by two neatly-dressed and well-spoken girls. When they had taken up their position—next to me, as it chanced— one of them said to the other, " And how's Ernest?" The second girl, not even lowering her voice, replied, a little petulantly, " He slept with me last night " . . . a statement so frank that it surprised me. I wondered if Ernest was perhaps a pekinese, but I realised that he was human when she continued, " You can't imagine ! We hadn't been together for some weeks and, my dear, he pawed and prodded the whole of my body, as if I were a piece of dough." Her companion murmured a few words of commiseration, and half a minute later the pair of them were boarding an omnibus and chattering about something else.

Girls, I daresay, have talked in this manner between themselves from the time of the cavemen ; but, hearing poor Ernest's enthusiasm described with complete disregard of the stranger who stood within a few inches of his unappreciative bedfellow, I perceived in a moment the astounding change in our view of sex that has occurred within the lifetime of a middle-aged man. It is even possible that she would not have surprised me if I had been her contemporary. At least I know that Rip van Winkle would have " stared and gasped " ; for the difference in sex outlook of this girl and the girl of 1900 is quite as profound as the difference in religious outlook of the modern man and the man of 1830.

III

WE should see our age very much more
clearly if the bodies of people did not
continually mislead us. Because of their bodies
we think of them as being young, middle-aged
and old; and knowing that the world is always
occupied by three generations, we are not at
all surprised that these three kinds of person
should be living here simultaneously. If we
could see them without their bodies, if we
could see them not as physical organisms but
as bundles of ideas, we should be as much
amazed as if some of them walked about in
chain-armour, some of them in frock-coats or
crinolines, and others in the dress of to-day.
For, looking at people mentally, we find that
they belong to dozens of different periods, and
the world takes on the variegated appearance
of a fancy-dress ball. Fundamentally, however,
we can divide them into three principal groups
—groups that are as distinct as geological strata.

First, there are the mediævally-minded—all
the many people who can adopt without dis-
comfort the religious ideas and the moral code

that were general in the days of Dante. They are quite unaffected by the discoveries which have altered the mind of man during the last five hundred years. They are still far more emotional than rational, and scientific knowledge is powerless to change them. It is not that they are intellectually dishonest, but rather that intellect in them does not demand to be satisfied before they can be emotionally comfortable. For the most part this group remains in the simple state of mind which Nelson and Wordsworth enjoyed. Most of them do not think at all, and are, indeed, not capable of weighing one probability against another. They continue throughout their lives to believe what they were told as children, and to walk about in the mental costume of an age that has long since passed. They are often kindly and usually virtuous, but, with the exception of the few that are genuine mystics, they are unquestionably a backward race. It is, indeed, as though there were people among us who still made knives by chipping flints.

The second group is immeasurably the largest. Here, in fact, are all the typical men and women of our time. It is made up of people who see plainly that two and two make four, who are unable to believe anything against the grain of their intellect, who are honestly surprised that anyone at so late a period should trouble his head about religion. To them religion is so obviously no more than a remnant of primitive superstition that they are exasperated by the slow-wittedness of the man who does not see this. They are the rationalists, the science-worshippers, the men and women who could no more believe that they are immortal than that they have wings to their ankles. It is difficult even to talk with them about any religious idea, for they instantly assume that anyone who does not agree with them must maintain a hundred and one ridiculous opinions; and it is quite impossible to make them realise that they themselves may represent a type which will some day seem as obsolete as the mediæval type.

And yet it may be so; for there is now a third group, which is composed of people who are not at all certain that religion is moonshine. They see well enough that science, having bombarded traditional religion for at least a century, has reduced it to a woeful ruin, and that no reasonable man could now share the outlook of Nelson and Wordsworth; but they also observe that science is no longer the down-right dogmatist that it was in the reigns of Huxley and Haeckel, and they go so far as to wonder, even, whether science, after all, is the sole illuminant which can show us a glimpse of the truth about ourselves. They suspect that the twentieth century will achieve a religion and a morality of its own, however simple, and are eager not to be left behind when that reconstruction begins. At the same time, they realise that the religion and morality of the near future will inevitably be as unlike those of our grandparents as Christianity was unlike Judaism. And since the mediævally-minded are contented with the ideas of a distant age and the scientifically-minded with the outlook of contemporary science, it is only to the members of this new group, which has lately emerged, that the point of view which I am about to present will not seem either needlessly intricate or ridiculously naïve.

IV

WE cannot even begin to think for ourselves until we appreciate the intense difficulty of doing so. Fashions in thought are as pervasive as fashions in attire. No gentleman in Dr. Johnson's time would have dreamed of appearing in public without a wig. To wear a periwig to-day is beyond the daring of any man. We smile, too, at the bustles which women wore in the 'eighties and at the long and massive skirts in which they attempted to play lawn-tennis in 1900; but the women did not feel that they were absurd, and few of them had courage enough to defy the tyranny of the modiste. Only custom, again, prevents us from recognising the ludicrous effect of plus-fours, though we may be quite confident that posterity will both marvel and mock.

Men, because their own clothes no longer change perceptibly in design, make fun of the slavishness with which women comply with each new fashion in dress; but they might restrain their amusement if they realised that they themselves are just as much the slaves of fashion in thought. A man's mind is not, as he imagines, his own. It is made up of conclusions about life which he has taken at tenth-hand from other men; for at no time are there more than a dozen men who can look out upon the world with their own eyes. Most of us do not think at all. We merely absorb the mental atmosphere that is around us.

Consider, for example, the millions who, until a generation ago, tormented themselves with the fear that they would not be " saved," with the terror that they might roast for ever in a supernatural furnace. Hell is now a reality to very few minds; and we look back with pity upon those generations of people, most of whom, like the poet Cowper, were exceptionally good and harmless, because they could not wake up and realise that they were the victims of what we are certain was nothing but an infantile nightmare. We can see clearly that their thoughts were communal—the mere handiwork of their period. Most of us, too, cannot help being astonished that Cardinal Newman, whose intelligence was of so high an order, could have turned round and round in a little cage of ideas that seem to us obviously fantastic, nor can we understand any better how Mr. Gladstone, accustomed to the handling of international affairs, could have been so much the slave of his generation that he spent a large part of his leisure in arguing that every syllable in the poetic story of Adam and Eve was literally true and divinely inspired. Moreover, I read quite lately a book in which two nimble-minded men engaged in a controversy about Jonah and the Whale; both of them taking the story with all solemnity, and one of them actually suggesting that, although whales have never been found in the Mediterranean, God was quite capable of putting one into it for the purpose of miraculously delivering Jonah from its belly. These illustrations clearly indicate that in most respects a man may be of his own time, but that in one or two matters he may be several centuries behind it.

We have no difficulty in perceiving the limitation of past minds. Everyone will acknowledge, for instance, that if he had been born when the great cathedrals of Europe were being built, he would have agitated himself about Nominalism and Realism or some other theological notion. Why is it, then, that we can no more argue gravely whether a whale did really swallow Jonah than we can lose our tempers over that classical problem of the Middle Ages— " how many angels can dance on the tip of a needle? " We do not trouble our minds with such fantasies because the spirit of science has completely altered the atmosphere in which we think. It is rarely, however, that anyone pauses to reflect that if he were living two hundred years hence he would again be thinking quite differently, and that his present thoughts might well seem to him as quaint as those which occupied the minds of men in the twelfth century.

The modern man who has no religion and only a vague morality is as much the child of his period as any hell-fearing evangelist. He no more realises why he is without a religion than why there are useless buttons on the sleeve of his coat. He has inherited both the buttons and the supposition that immortality was merely a day-dream. When we read of the intellectual nightmare that ruined Cowper's life, we feel—almost with impatience—" Why couldn't the poor man shake it off and recognise, as we do, that it was all unreal? " The answer is obvious—that he could not get out of the atmosphere around him; but we do not apply this reflection to ourselves. The intellectuals of to-day are as confident in their scepticism as the evangelicals once were in their beliefs. They cannot see that they are as closely imprisoned within the present limits of scientific orthodoxy as their great-grandfathers were within the limits of orthodox theology; or that the men of the future will pity them because they were not bolder and more independent of their age, precisely as we ourselves pity the people who went through their lives in dread of hell-fire.

V

LET us see, then, why it is that most of our contemporaries are reasonably certain that neither God nor the soul exists. Let us trace, in fact, the lineage of that outlook upon life which we naïvely suppose that we have attained by our own thought and judgment. It is not a new outlook. We are told that no people was ever more intensely religious than the ancient Hindus; and yet I remember, out of my youthful reading, that there was in India, even at a very early period, a materialistic school of philosophy. It is obvious, too, that the Roman stoics, though they lacked our scientific knowledge, had no more belief in an after-life than most of us have ourselves; but, as everyone knows, just at the time when the stoics had achieved their noblest expression, the mind of the world mysteriously changed. Christianity, rapidly spreading across the Roman Empire, made men more confident than ever before that they were spiritual and immortal beings, until, after a thousand years, we see that the mind of European man is moving in what we may call the Mediæval Dream. In the course of many generations that dream became exceedingly complex, as anyone will discover if he explores a few volumes of theology; but it is possible to suggest in outline how life and the universe then appeared to those of our ancestors who were immersed in that dream.

They assumed that the earth was the centre of the universe, just as the Babylonian map-makers assumed that Babylon was the central point on a flat world; and in this dream-view the sun, the moon and the stars had been set up and lighted in the firmament by the hands of God in order that they might help mankind and adorn the astonishing picture at which men gaze. Moreover, men and women were manifestly the most important inhabitants of the visible universe. Indeed, whenever a baby was born, God created a new and immortal soul which He placed inside it, and thenceforth that soul was answerable to God for its actions. Nor could it plead that it was uncertain whether an action was right or wrong. The dreamers had drawn up, for instance, a list of the Seven Deadly Sins. And life itself was only a brief prelude to an everlasting existence either above the earth, in heaven, or below it, in hell. A man, therefore, was a creature of great importance.

Nothing whatsoever was more precious than his soul. The Good Spirit and the Evil Spirit within the universe contended with one another for possession of it.

The dream persisted for so long that humanity used some centuries in the effort to wake up from it. Indeed, there are still some people who have not waked up, and only a generation ago there was a very large number. Among the earliest of the minds that began to stir uneasily was Copernicus, who demonstrated that the earth was not the centre of all things. Happily for their self-respect, very few of the dreamers foresaw the implications of this discovery, and those few resisted it strongly. The mind of man, however, was imperceptibly entering upon a new phase—the phase of intellectuality—and slowly, as generations went by, an increasing minority began to see that the new doctrine had to be digested. It is easy to imagine the disquiet with which they pondered the idea that the earth, after all, was merely like a pebble on the shore of an immeasurable sea. They must inevitably have wondered whether men had been thinking too grandly about themselves. Most men, they could see, were like children in a nursery who are preoccupied with their own minute circle of interests and entirely incapable of realising the insignificance of the nursery compared with the tumultuous world beyond it. Those who had absorbed the Copernican idea were like children who have just gone to school. In them the intense egoism of childhood had cracked, like an eggshell, and they had painfully to adjust themselves to a larger world in which they were no longer quite so important.

Men, on the whole, continued to move within the Mediæval Dream, and they were not to feel the true force of the Copernican idea until certain other pronouncements of science had roused them to a greater uneasiness. We have seen how Nelson and Wordsworth, who are not far away from us in time, could still assume that God was paying special attention to their affairs. And yet even in Wordsworth's time geologists had begun to trouble the sleepers. The evidence of the earth, they said, and of the creatures which it had once entombed, could not be reconciled with the hallowed declaration of Bishop Usher that God created the world on a certain day of the year 4004 B.C. Even so, there was an eminent dreamer who tried to reassure the sleepy by suggesting that God had deposited those fossilised animals at various depths of the earth in order to test the faith of his children; but by this time a sufficiently large number of men had waked up to render the acceptance of such a fantasy impossible, and Bishop Usher's calculation, in which Cromwell and Milton had believed, was quietly tipped into the dustbin. The question of the earth's age was not, it is true, a matter which could greatly trouble the emotions of men. Nevertheless, this new revelation was another landmark in the emergence of reason. It caused men to doubt the Biblical story of Creation. It showed that the Bible did not contain all knowledge and was not completely reliable.

And then—so late as the middle of the last century—came the terrific repercussions of Darwin's disinterested inquiry into *The Origin of Species* and *The Descent of Man*. We have long since recovered from the nasty shock of hearing that we are descended from monkeys, or at least that men and monkeys diverged from a common ancestor: and it is therefore almost impossible for anyone who is now under forty to realise how severe a blow this announcement gave to the self-respect of our grandfathers; how it seemed to take half the relish out of life for the meditative man; how strenuously, how passionately and, in the end, how desperately the old type of mind, ingeniously putting together its theological toy, resisted the Darwinian idea; how much dismay, perturbation and sorrow that doctrine caused; or how thousands of worthy people prayed that Darwin might see the Light and recant his abominable doctrine or, alternatively, die speedily before he could spread it any further. That is now an old tragedy. People felt that if they were to admit a kinship between men and monkeys, they would have to abandon the inspiring idea that God created man in his own image and placed into every baby's body an immortal soul; but no matter how strenuously the dreamers might try to disregard the alarum-clock, time was against them. Men could not fall asleep again, and within a generation or two the whole civilised world had inured itself to the humiliating implications of "evolution."

By this time—about sixty years ago—the belief which had supported Nelson and Wordsworth was in a precarious condition. It lingered, as it lingers even now, in a diminishing number of those who were born with mediæval minds; but in the eighteen-seventies the man of the future was the militant rationalist who no longer stopped half-way, but proceeded to preach with fervour against the doctrines of the Mediæval Dream. The man of this type might have taken as his own Bible a noble-minded, sad-hearted, resolutely rationalistic book—*The Martyrdom of Man*, by Winwood Reade: a complete expression of the sorrow and the courage with which men abandoned the dream that had held them for nearly two thousand years.

Huxley called himself an agnostic, or one who does not know. The transition to thoroughgoing materialism was easy and inevitable; and Haeckel, no doubt, would have called himself a materialist, or one who denies that there is anything immaterial in man or in the universe. This view achieved its ultimate expression when a German scientist affirmed that "the brain secretes mind as the liver secretes bile." Gradually, under the influence of such writers, who never lacked confidence, and later of literary men (for instance, Matthew Arnold), and later still of newspaper-writers, a larger and larger multitude of new minds began in early youth to assume that their grandfathers had lived in a fool's paradise: and it was in a generally de-christianised atmosphere that those of us who are now middle-aged became young men.

In 1900 the change was apparent in "advanced" circles, but it had not percolated into general society. At that time, when I was still struggling with the reports of Xenophon and Julius Cæsar, the simple outlook of Nelson and Wordsworth was maintained by the people among whom I lived. Each day before breakfast, for instance, we assembled—together with the cook, the parlourmaid, the housemaid and the scullery-girl—for Family Prayers: a Victorian institution which I suppose to have become exceedingly uncommon. The ceremony had little effect upon me, for my head was always full of the cricket scores which I had hurriedly absorbed from the Family Newspaper, and I think that even for my father it was really a formal proceeding. A typical Victorian of the gentler kind, he undoubtedly believed in God and in prayer and in salvation, but these Family Prayers, I am confident, were little more to him than a custom which he had carried over from my grandfather's régime. And the men who came to the house were mostly lawyers, antiquarians and stockbrokers. I do not say that they were at all devout. Nevertheless, like the immense majority of old or middle-aged persons in 1900, they did adhere, however unreflectingly, to the basic ideas of the Mediæval Dream. Indeed, my uncle Belfort Bax, a socialist and philosopher of some note in his day, was the only visitor to the house who was not a churchman or a chapel-goer. In short, the ideas of Darwin and his apostles had not, even then, seriously upset the mind of the ordinary citizen.

On the other hand, as I have already hinted, the Darwinian doctrines had been at work for some forty years in the world of the "intellectuals," and when I began to enter their world, about 1903, I found myself among men and women who were a second generation of sceptics. They smiled indulgently at the late Lord Tennyson's timid "doubts" concerning "the creeds"; they went, in a crusading spirit, to the performances of the Stage Society on Sunday evenings; and the most up-to-date of their representatives—a certain Bernard Shaw—had already horrified the orthodox with his "handbook of diabolonian ethics" and his taunts at family life.

These latter-day agnostics had endured no agony of conscience. Their agnosticism had come to them, if not with their mother's milk, at least in their adolescence. They assumed, in a kind of freemasonry, that the soul was a pathetic myth and that God was no more than a colossal shadow thrown across the universe by the puzzled figure of primitive man. Unlike their fathers, they never argued these matters. I, who was then an excited materialist, very greatly wished that they would; but I soon realised that they looked upon the discussion of any religious conception as intellectual bad form: and most of them diverted into socialism the altruistic emotions that arose from their submerged religious instinct.

Meanwhile the anthropologists had been widening the breach that Darwin had made in that state of mind which was still general in 1850. Sir James Frazer's magnificent work *The Golden Bough*, for instance, did much to extract the last remnants of religion from the atmosphere of our century. His work was read by thousands. The effect of it was felt by millions. The thousands believed that they had seen the very origins of religion and morality exposed and discredited. Frazer, and others, appeared to have proved that all religious notions could be traced back to the efforts of savages to control the external world by means of more or less ridiculous magical ceremonies. He showed, even, that there was nothing unique in the Crucifixion and the Resurrection; that innumerable tribes of primitive men had persuaded themselves that they could benefit their crops by " killing the god," and that humanity, from almost its earliest days, had dramatised the death of the world in winter and its resurrection in spring.

The thinking section of society was now rid of all the old preconceptions. Wordsworth and Nelson were completely out-moded. There was, as it were, an open market for new philosophies; and every three or four years a new philosophy duly demanded the attention of those who had no religion. What with scientific materialism, pragmatism, creative evolutionism, behaviourism, relativity and all the other competing interpretations of mind or matter, it is small wonder if the average man, who spent most of his time in gaining a livelihood, became thoroughly bewildered, and shirked the investigation of so many philosophies, and decided to drift, as he is drifting now, in a vague scepticism.

Finally, as though to extinguish religion for good, the Freudian system of psycho-analysis reached, at long last, the reeling intellect of the average man. Here was a map of the mind so brilliantly set forth that for some years it excited intelligent and semi-intelligent people as though it were a final revelation of truth. Journalists exploited it because they saw at once that it was based upon the idea that from birth to death men and women are swayed and moulded by sexual instinct. That first excitement has lapsed already. Society women no longer discuss " the Oedipus Complex " or the condition of their libido; and literary critics, under the influence of fashion, have now begun actually to reprimand a writer who still makes use, as he should, of Freud's revelations. Freud, it seemed, had applied " the bare bodkin " to the old conception of " God," for God was now seen by the intellectuals to be only a magnified image of a child's physical father or even of "the old man" in a group of apes. We were said, also, to be haunted by an image of paradise or by a yearning for a far-distant Golden Age because the mind, being exposed to a hostile world, longs to recover the effortless existence which an embryo was assumed to enjoy in its mother's womb.

In the manner of their kind the intellectuals of 1900 were a little ahead of their period. By comparison with the undevout but church-going lawyers and stockbrokers, they were few in number; but they belonged to the future. They were thinking as the ordinary citizen was destined to think in 1930: and it is they, especially the literary men among them, who are chiefly responsible for creating so sceptical an atmosphere that a young man in 1930, far from fighting his way out of religious dogmas, never considers them seriously at all. If we think of those who were literary leaders in 1900 we shall see that the Wordsworthian conception of a man as a spiritual being is replaced by a quiet assumption that scientific materialism is the only wear for a self-respecting mind. Anatole France, for example, delighted the intellectuals of that period with his ironic treatment of the mediævally-minded. Bernard Shaw, who has always been journalistically sensitive to the feeling of the immediate future, perceived very early that traditional religion, for all its appearance of strength, was a lost cause. H. G. Wells, excited in youth by the scientific revelation, has never outgrown, it seems, the assumption that religion is negligible because one crystallised form of it was broken to pieces when he was beginning to think. Bennett and Galsworthy, at least in my judgment, are obviously writers who merely took the tone of their age as a schoolboy will take the tone of his public-school. These authors, and a hundred others, have done more than any man may calculate to produce a mental atmosphere in which materialism comes easily to an opening mind; but with no disrespect to them we may doubt whether they would have looked at life as they do if they had been contemporaries of Abelard or Dante or even of Dickens and Thackeray. In a word, they have not themselves made any discovery that invalidates a belief in God or the soul. They have merely disseminated an attitude of mind which derives from the work of half a dozen scientists; but so great has been their influence that it is now difficult for an average man to hold the balances fairly between religion and materialism. And yet if we are to think clearly, and not to be carried along by the tide of one particular age, we must realise the history of our prejudices and inclinations, understand that we are not judging life independently, and acknowledge that we look at it through the minds of Copernicus, Darwin, Huxley, Haeckel, Frazer, Freud, and all those effective writers whom these scientific men in turn have influenced.

At this point, then, let us see how the average man, absorbing the atmosphere of our age, regards the universe, his own nature and the certainty of oncoming death.

WE may pretend as we will, but the truth is that modern knowledge is decidedly disheartening. No matter which way we turn our minds, we shall find something to humiliate us. The universe (let us confess it frankly) is inhospitably vast, and we ourselves are depressingly minute. When the astronomer has talked to us about billions of miles, billions of years, billions of stars, and when we have done our best to imagine it all, we do realise that the universe is indeed mysterious—that it could not be more mysterious than it is, not though it were a palace in a story told by Scheherazade —but we also totter to the bathroom and absent-mindedly dress for dinner with a melancholy sense of human insignificance. And when the astronomer ruthlessly suggests, in his airy way, that life itself may have started accidentally: this very life which has involved us in all these wonderings about death: why, then we may readily marvel that anyone should attach the slightest importance to any human affairs. In that mood we may go about with a detestable suspicion that we are all just momentary cheesemites in a little round cheese that ridiculously bowls along through space. Even the wars of the world—and there can hardly have been five years at a stretch during which there was no war in any part of it—will then seem almost as comical as they had hitherto seemed tragic; and the now dismal student of astronomy may look back with astonishment upon the violent emotions with which he doubted, an hour or two earlier, the chastity of the cheesemite who is his wife.

To the university-minded man, whose thoughts and emotions are as distinct as oil and water, astronomy is perhaps only a matter of interesting calculations; but the normal man, who applies to life any scraps of knowledge that he can acquire and in whom, therefore, thought and knowledge turn instantly into emotion, is likely to derive from an acquaintance with Light Years and the Milky Way nothing but a conviction that neither his life nor his behaviour is of any importance at all. Transformed, as he now feels, into an almost invisible mannikin,—thoroughly crushed, in fact,—he will see humanity as a growing child who has now had the pretty nonsense knocked out of him and for whom the years of delighted make-believe are over. And then he will try to forget all about it, wishing—unless his passion for pure knowledge is quite exceptional—that the Inquisition had arisen in time to send Copernicus literally to blazes. Then at least he might still be able to think of himself as an immortal spirit in whom the Architect of the Universe took a lively interest. As it is, he directs his energy outwards, hoping to snatch a little pleasure from his handful of years, or studying, to amuse or assuage his ravenous intellect, the forces and appearances of the physical world.

Or perhaps, being determined to regain his natural cheerfulness, he seeks an emollient in Nature,—beautiful Nature who has inspired the best work of so many appreciative poets and painters. No one can deny that in Nature there is boundless beauty for our human senses—beauty of colour, line, texture, perfume and even sound: but what will he think of her " marvellous adaptation " whereby one creature is curiously equipped with the means of killing another—often, if not always, to an accompaniment of keen pain? Once, on a hill in the quiet Cotswolds, I watched a weasel sinuously leaping after an unobservant rabbit until, with a final spring, it fixed its teeth in the nape of the squeaking rabbit's neck. Once, in a book by Fabre, I read (but long ago, and I may be at fault in detail) how the glow-worm is provided by Mother Nature with a

48

special acid which it injects into a snail, with the happy result that the snail is reduced to a liquid upon which the glow-worm feeds. And in a remarkable treatise on Buddhism,[1] I find the following passage: " Consider, for example, the case of the ' Killer-Whale '— the smallest animal of its family; and the fashion wherein it treats the vastly larger member of its own family—the huge sperm-whale. Attacking it with continuous blows of its tail, again and again the Killer tries to dislocate the jaw of its huge victim by seizing and pulling it downward as, with opened mouth, the great creature strives to escape. Often the unequal combat lasts for two or three whole days and nights; until the great sperm-whale is exhausted and, despite its former strength, no more can close its mouth against the horrible attack of the ferocious Killer. Then, pulling with all its might, the Killer succeeds in dislocating the sperm-whale's lower jaw, so that it can no more close its mouth. Then the Killer reaps the reward of its long combat. Entering the huge animal's mouth, it eats out its tongue—and departs to leave the hapless monster to die in a slow torment of agony and starvation."

Hundreds of comparable instances could be

[1] *The Wisdom of the Aryas*, by Allan Bennett. (Kegan Paul, Trench, Trübner & Co.)

given, no doubt, by qualified students; and in place of Wordsworth's view of Nature as the revelation of a beautiful and all-powerful intelligence, the modern man is left to share Tennyson's horror of " Nature red in tooth and claw," and from Tennyson, who, as usual, stopped halfway, he may easily progress to the view of Thomas Hardy, who felt that the whole order of Nature, in which we are included, could have been devised and set in motion by nothing except an abominable and fiendish imagination.

Already the modern man, remembering those innumerable suns in space, will find some difficulty in believing that God, if responsible for their activities, can seriously have supervised Aunt Sarah's illness or even the Battle of Trafalgar. He will also find difficulty in believing that the inventor of Nature's processes can be wholly benign. God, in fact, will have become to his mind an exceedingly shadowy and improbable conception. When, therefore, he next looks at the history of his own race, he feels that his scepticism concerning God and the soul has been vigorously confirmed. Every history-book, of those which I know, is a monument to " man's inhumanity to man." We could fill the Vatican Library with records of human cruelty, trickery and injustice. Indeed, I have been convinced for many years that nobody can imagine any abomination which has not been practised by members of our race; and if anyone were to question this view, I should recommend him to re-read a chapter in *The Brothers Karamazov*, where one of the characters has made a list of the most outrageous life-stories that had come to his hearing. Alternatively, we need only examine Gibbon's *Decline and Fall* or Green's *Short History of the English People* to realise how often unscrupulous villains have occupied positions of power, and how few are the heroes in history compared with the long procession of human devils.

There is danger in citing particular instances,—the danger of forgetting that they are not exceptional instances of human depravity and of the loathsome injustice to which forgotten men—and women—were forced to submit: and yet, without some illustration of the atrocities which human beings have inflicted and suffered, we incline to forget the continual craft and cruelty which have disgraced humanity throughout its record. Consider, then, how—not a century ago—hungry immigrants to America were fighting violently for the body of a dead rat, and how on at least one occasion they devoured the dead bodies of their fellow-passengers. Consider how ingeniously the Chinese have tortured their victims,—though indeed we require to have seen their instruments, as I have, before we can appreciate the fiendishness of those that used them. Consider, again, the perfidy of Richard the Second toward the Kentish rebels; the vile abuse of power which Domitian exercised when, in order to secure Julia, he directed the murder of her husband, who had offended in no way; and the behaviour of Queen Fredegond, who, finding her daughter bent over a chest, banged down the lid upon the girl's neck and so attempted to strangle her. Remember the wholesale butcheries of Ivan the Terrible. Remember the famous metal bull which the Sicilian tyrant caused to be constructed; how, when it had been made red-hot, he would have his victims thrust into it from behind, enjoying the subsequent noises that resounded from the bull's throat. And if these memories are not enough to sicken us of our kind, we may try the effect of reading the following passage, quoted from Addington Symonds, about the blood-lust of Ibrahim ibn Ahmed, prince of Africa and Sicily (A.D. 875): "This man, besides displaying peculiar ferocity in his treatment of enemies and prisoners of war, delighted in the execution of horrible butcheries within the walls of his own palace. His astrologers having once predicted that he should die by the hands of a 'small assassin,' he killed off the whole retinue of his pages and filled up their places with a suite of negroes, whom he proceeded to treat after the same fashion. On another occasion, when one of his three hundred eunuchs had by chance been witness of the tyrant's drunkenness, Ibrahim slaughtered the whole band. Again, he is said to have put an end to sixty youths, originally selected for his pleasures, burning them by gangs of five or six in the furnace, or suffocating them in the hot chambers of his baths. . . . But his fiercest fury was directed against women. . . . Wives and concubines were strangled, sawn asunder, and buried alive, if they showed signs of pregnancy. His female children were murdered as soon as they saw the light; sixteen of them, whom his mother managed to conceal and rear at her own peril, were massacred upon the spot when Ibrahim discovered whom they claimed as father. . . . One of the most marked symptoms (of his disease) was the curiosity which led him to explore the entrails of his victims, and to feast his eyes upon their quivering hearts. After causing his first minister Ibn-Semsâma to be beaten to death, he cut his body open, and with his own knife sliced the brave man's heart. On another occasion he had five hundred prisoners brought before him. Seizing a sharp lance he first explored the region of their ribs, and then plunged the spear-point into the heart of each victim in succession. A garland of these hearts was made and hung up on the gate of Tunis." Nero, compared with this monster, becomes almost an amiable figure, for he was at least an artist, a man of some sensibility; but Ivan the Terrible is, unfortunately, not the only tyrant whose treatment of other men bears some resemblance to that of Ibrahim: and if we wish to maintain a belief that there is an immortal principle in man, we must reckon, using all the imagination which we possess, with the very worst that we can discover in human history. Our belief, to be worth anything, must be hardy, no hot-house plant, no nursling of sentimentality and a sheltered life in a highly-civilised community. We must, in a word, be able to account for Ibrahim ibn Ahmed and Ivan the Terrible.

The profound religious instinct which we inherit from hundreds of generations, an instinct which has outlived not only the huge cavalcade of history but the even huger stretches of time which we call pre-history, would have had difficulty in withstanding the impact of our knowledge concerning astronomy, Nature and human affairs. In the average man, however, it had already been stunned by the theory of evolution and again by the shrewd blows of the anthropologist. He knows, for example, that the human embryo rapidly recapitulates the development of the human body from a series of sub-human forms. In the bathroom, too, he can feel the stump of his vestigial tail. He is therefore strongly disposed to think that a human being is just a super-animal; one who has specialised in brain-improvement and who, in consequence, has added greatly to the instinctive cunning of the other animals. And when he looks round at the other humans, he thinks inevitably that they are very queer immortals.

We must admit the difficulty of discerning any immortal essence in a sea-side landlady; in the elderly ladies and gentlemen at a boarding-house who seem to be little more than dummies or digestive machines; or in the silly faces of shop-gazing women and the coarse faces of men at a prize-fight. Nor is the immortal spirit more apparent in the society woman whose mind is chiefly occupied in impressing other women with her social superiority and in doctoring her face and body: or in the groups of financiers who, from time to time, callously float schemes that inflict ruin and misery upon thousands of their brother-creatures; or in the ruffian who, having gravely wounded a policeman, will deliberately shoot out his victim's eyes. These, if immortal, are very queer indeed; and the modern man will think to himself that it was all very well for people in pre-scientific days—for Nelson and Wordsworth, for Newman and Gladstone—to fancy that God placed an immortal spirit, a slip of his own divinity, into the body of each baby as it drew its first breath: but he cannot persuade himself that an imperishable essence is conjured out of the vasty deep when, on a Saturday night, a drunken lout and a syphilitic trollop succeed in mingling their bodies. He feels, on the contrary, that nothing more august or mysterious has happened on that occasion than during the casual union of a boar and a sow in the stye or of two cats on the house-tops. And what of the clergyman's daughter, from some quiet rectory, who debauched her body on a table in Rouen, during the War, for the satisfaction of a platoon? What of the girl at a recent artists' ball in Paris who lay, drunken and exposed, on another table and whose body was sexually used by a passing dancer who had nothing better to do? We know, upon Wordsworth's authority, that

" the heavens themselves have goings-on,"

but these are not the actions which we should expect of spiritual beings, nor can we convince ourselves that another spiritual being could, by chance, be generated in so casual a manner. And next, though perhaps not consciously, the modern man advances to the feeling that, if we are not immortal souls, then humanity was merely playing a fantastic game with its own mind when it tried to exalt marriage—and the sexual union which marriage implies—into a sacrament. When a man and a woman were thought to be evoking an immortal spirit into existence, they were also thought to be engaged in a high and serious enterprise. When, on the contrary, we do not believe their offspring to be an immortal, sexual union loses of necessity its importance, its nobility, its very seriousness. And here, in fact, is a leading cause of the sexual laxity which characterises our period.

For some years it was customary to ascribe every social decline or change to " the War ": but the sceptical spirit, and sexual laxity also, were unmistakable from the beginning of our century. The War merely speeded them up, as it speeded up the development of flying. Nevertheless, the War did suppress the last flutterings of the antique religious instinct in many thousands of people, and alike in the simple and the sophisticated. A studio-model, a girl of seventeen (her name was Topsy), startled me once, when she was posing on a day in the early months of the War, by saying quietly, " I don't believe in God any longer.

If there were a God, He wouldn't allow the War to go on." And what of the men who were in the thick of it? Some that I knew did not doubt that they and their comrades would exist after death; but I am never surprised when a soldier who has witnessed that loathsome and idiotic carnage tells me that he is an out-and-out materialist. The man who has watched a shell, let loose by men who could not see their victims, obliterate this man and that, in an instant, as heedlessly as some persons will smudge out the life of a harmless insect; whose own cannons have made such an uproar, for six or seven hours on end, that he could not hear the explosion of the hostile shells and observed them only by reason of the " brown fountains " of earth which they created; who has had to retire with his company and has passed a whole group of men " pounded into the earth like raisins in dough," and has been conscious of the raw-meat stench that they and others exuded: such a man will not think it probable that a kindly and all-seeing God was presiding over the destinies of these luckless fellows—each of them the laborious product of nine months' work in the womb and some twenty years in the world—or that they were anything more than a collection of insects whose bodies and intelligences had been extinguished at random.

It would be absurd to suppose that the average man, who is so much preoccupied with fighting the world for his livelihood, consciously recalls these various influences upon his outlook. For the most part he is not aware of them: but they are, as we say, in the air, and it is they that make it hard for him to believe that there is any purpose, or even any sense, in the complicated scene upon which he looks, or that he himself or anyone whom he loves has the smallest likelihood of surviving the drastic effect of death.

VII

THERE have been other periods of intellectual and moral confusion as pronounced as ours; but no bygone generation has had to grapple with so much knowledge. Even when we say that a man is a scientist, we mean only that he is well acquainted with certain branches of science and, perhaps, that his mind is oriented in a particular way. And these men alone—these whom we call scientists—propound their theories, make their discoveries of fact, and contradict one another, so rapidly that we soon despair of keeping pace with them. That, indeed, is why most of us are completely bewildered, and some of us tragically: for everywhere, though they may not say as much, there are young men and women who, finding no ready-made niches in the world and having caught from the spirit of the age a supposition that they are merely intelligent animals, feel themselves to be useless, and think, in secret, that they might just as well rid society of at least one futile cheesemite.

Moreover, it may well be this medley of doctrines that has caused many intelligent people of a different type to throw aside all modern science, as we throw aside an intractable crossword puzzle, and to find consolation in the outlook of the Middle Ages. " Men do not want to be free," said the great Italian dictator, and although he was thinking of political freedom, his simple and startling words apply just as truly to freedom of speculation.

Most modern men, however, cannot go back to a mediæval philosophy. They could as easily believe in dryads or fairies or in the gods and goddesses of Homeric Greece. And yet how timid and how thoughtless are those who prostrate themselves abjectly before the Juggernaut Car of contemporary science! The first duty of any scientist is to advance with the utmost caution, as the first duty of a priest is to behave with the utmost circumspection: but one thing is quite certain—that scientific knowledge will continue to expand. The men of 2000 A.D. will know more than we know. They may even know that death does not snuff out a man's consciousness: and those who dare not out-run the scientific pronouncements of our generation should recall how Huxley once confidently asserted that an atom was indestructible, and that every atom in the universe had existed in precisely the same form from the beginning of time. His successors appear to have proved that he was wrong, but the science-worshippers of his day accepted the statement as an important truth.

The constitution of an atom is not, of course, a subject which has any effect upon our emotions or our behaviour. Professors might fly at each other's throats about it, but the layman, if he was ever aware of Huxley's mistake, has long since overlooked it as a trifling error. The problem of human immortality is a very different matter. If science had already announced that there is indubitably a God in the universe and that we are indubitably spiritual and immortal beings, and that Huxley was mistaken in these matters too, our emotions and our behaviour would be fundamentally affected. The whole of life would look different. If, then, we have any common sense, we shall not wait for science to make certain of every inch that we travel. Our lives may well be over before it has assured men, as it may, that they are, after all, immortal, though for a long time they dared not think so. What we need and desire is a view of life, a philosophy, by which we can steer our conduct; by which, whether with stoical resignation or with hope and a high heart, we may face the apparent extinction of death:

and, while we are watching science advance with due caution, we ought to make a philosophy, however speculative, for ourselves. Otherwise, we are spiritless victims of an age, a generation or a mere decade.

PART II

I

I COULD not tell you how many times I have seen a pitying smile creep up the face of my collocutor when he hears me admit that I believe in the survival of the soul. I am never permitted to refine upon this intimation. Indeed, I have often not been able to finish a first sentence; for one and all, these collocutors have jumped to a hundred suppositions. Some have explained that I could not entertain this old-fashioned notion if I had taken the trouble to read Darwin, Huxley, Haeckel or Sir James Jeans; others have said kindly that I ought to study the works of Sigmund Freud; others, again, have merely murmured the names of a few anthropologists and then turned away, as though I were manifestly so primitive that to educate me would involve many years of hard work; and a few, snorting brightly, have remarked, " But of course you have never considered the new conception of time." One and all, they instantly docketed me as a quaint specimen of the Nelsonian and Wordsworthian stratum.

It is true that, unlike so many persons, I have not read everything; but when I was seventeen I had an acute attack of intellectuality and listened to the materialistic philosophers with reverence. Moreover, I can remember how I read certain works on psychology, works which then were new and authoritative, and that in most of these I learned that all mental or emotional " phenomena," including dreams, could be explained physiologically. I imagine that any psychologist who should attribute all dreams now—nearly thirty years later—to indigestion, or a noise in the street, or the slipping down of a blanket would be asked to retire on a pension. At the time, though, anyone who doubted whether dreams could be so simply explained would have been treated with the pity and contempt which now greet a suggestion that consciousness may, after all, outlast death: but the man who prides himself upon being up to date conveniently forgets a bygone orthodoxy.

The commonest rebuke to an immortalist is the wholly unwarranted statement that he believes in immortality because he wishes to live for ever. Many people assume that a man could not desert from the cheerless philosophy of materialism for any other reason. But can we really be certain that every man at all times would sooner be immortal than perishable? I am not at all sure that we can. Most people, no doubt, would sympathise with an ageing poet who said, the other day, " I hate getting old and knowing that I shall soon have to leave this lovely world ": but there are many people who find the world—or human life, at least,—very far from lovely, and many whom life tires out and who have had enough of it some years before it releases them. There are more than a few, as I know from experience, who could wish for nothing better than to be able to say with confidence,

> " Then star nor sun shall waken,
>   Nor any change of light:
> Nor sound of waters shaken,
>   Nor any sound or sight:
> Nor wintry leaves nor vernal,
>   Nor days nor things diurnal;
> Only the sleep eternal
>   In an eternal night."

And if it is by no means always a love of life that makes a man believe in immortality, neither is it a craven terror of death. In civilised countries most people would say, with the death-haunted poet John Ford,[1]

> " Death? Pish! 'tis but a sound; a name of air;
> A minute's storm, or not so much. . . . To tumble
> From bed to bed, be massacred alive
> By some physicians, for a month or two,

---

[1] In the last scene of *Perkin Warbeck*.

In hope of freedom from a fever's torments,
Might stagger manhood. . . . Here, the pain is past
Ere sensibly 'tis felt, . . ."

lines which, though unhappily not always applicable, are true enough of a normal death : " a minute's storm, or not so much." Most people, too, will recognise the wisdom and the consolation of Cicero's remark, " At death we either pass into a better state or we become nothing. If the former is true, we have nothing to fear. If the latter is true, we shall not know it."

Even those who relish living, those who rejoice in " this lovely world," would admit that death takes from most people as much of pain, anxiety and disappointment as of pleasure. And although Dr. Johnson was probably right, if we except the martyrs, when he said bluntly that every man is afraid of death, we shall see that it is not the whole man but only one part of him which has an inevitable dread of extinction. At first thought, indeed, it is strange that we should be so timorously preoccupied with an event which has come to every man since man first walked—an event, also, which is taking place each moment of each day in one part or another of the world. If we try to imagine the incalculable multitudes who have died—and they must be as many as the grains of sand on this planet—we shall see that to be afraid of death is almost ludicrous: for nothing will happen to us which has not happened to many millions of other men who were once alive and thinking.

II

THERE must be ten thousand books on "sex," on religion, on anthropology, on biology, and in fact on every province of knowledge into which I shall stray; and if I attempted to write as an expert I should be as ridiculous as an amateur billiard-player who fatuously decided to compete with professionals. If I began to quote high authorities I should need to quote five hundred, and for this reason I shall not quote any.

Some people enjoy a serene and constant certitude that the dead have, as the Japanese used to put it, merely "changed their world"; but I must admit to having moments of intellectuality when I wonder if, after all, I am deceiving myself; if, after all, it is likely that I should be right and so many of my learned or sharp-witted contemporaries be wrong; if, after all, the past can possibly be destined to triumph over the present. That, of course, is the mood upon which most modern men rely. We differ in this—that I distrust a mood of mere intellectuality, regarding it as a contraction of the mind, and that they distrust any other mood.

If, then, I believed in the extinction of consciousness, I should still find a pleasure of imagination in knowing that I shared my position with two men so noble of nature as Marcus Aurelius and Seneca; but again and again, looking at the question as honestly as I can, I find that for me it is impossible to feel sure that death is an everlasting eclipse. If I wished it to be so, I could not think it.

Now, I have come to a stage of life at which death and a man are seldom strangers; nor could I even say how many people are dead with whom I have exchanged ideas or shared experiences. During the very month in which I began to pen these pages, the newspapers announced the death of two persons whom I expected to see again and often: H. D., a pretty girl who was drowned in a wild sea, and P. T., a gay and sweet-natured woman who was killed in a motor-car disaster. And only last year died Arnold Bennett, whom I had assumed I should know for many years. There is no question about it, they, and all those others who died earlier, do seem definitely to be gone: and I never hear of a friend's death without experiencing the sensation of emptiness which comes to us when a liner glides away and we can no longer distinguish the hand that was waving farewell. But that—to be honest—is exactly what I do feel: that he has gone to strange and unknown conditions, and that I am left behind among familiar things. I remember that sensation coming to me in great strength one day, very early in the Great War, while I was walking along Regent Street. Thousands of young men, German, French and English, had lately been killed in a battle; and to me it seemed queer not that they should suddenly be out of this world, but that I and all the men and women about me should still be looking at shops, omnibuses and a September sky, still be thinking of meals and how to pay bills and whether our bodies were comfortable or not. It was the living, the left-behind, who seemed to me ghostly, not the dead.

Consider, too, that anyone from whom mysterious death has abruptly withdrawn a really loved friend is in no mood for make-believe. The contrary is true. Then at least we have to be honest with ourselves. We could as easily pretend, after an accident, that he had not broken his leg as that he still exists when we are inwardly certain that he does not. Far from causing us to rush, like alarmed children, to the comfort of ideas which are untenable, the disappearance of a friend makes us examine more scrupulously than ever our deep suspicions about the effect of death. At those times I have never been able to assure myself that he is " nowhere and nothing." I feel only (if I may vary my illustration) that a change has removed him beyond my present reach: as if he had driven away very fast in a car, and I were left powerless to communicate with him for the simple reason that my voice will not carry a mile.

Nothing, of course, can stop the emotional pain which we feel when a friend has died; but, whatever our philosophical view may be, we can alleviate it a little by remembering to be as glad that he ever lived, and that luck or destiny enabled us to know him, as we are grieved that he has now vanished beyond the radius of our life-limited perception.

III

THE world is strangely divided in its verdict upon psychic phenomena, and with how strange a ferocity do men of a certain kind resent the suggestion that they may not be wholly mortal! Are they always noble specimens of intellectual incorruptibility? Or do some of them so vehemently repel any attempt to prove the survival of consciousness because, if they were forced to accept that view, they would have completely to rearrange their minds? The confident sceptic assumes that his opponent clings to the old belief about the soul simply because he dare not face the thought of extinction; but it may be that sceptics resist the idea of an " after-life " mostly because, like children, they are afraid of the dark and of the unknown. My knowledge of mediumship is practically negligible. I take it, however, that any sensible person would agree that most mediums are shams. Only a few months ago Mr. Justice Cluer informed the world that " spiritualism is all quackery "; and yet, while he was giving

us that assurance, somewhere in England Sir
Oliver Lodge was at work—Sir Oliver, who
has no doubt whatever that the dead and the
living have communicated. If Mr. Justice
Cluer, as we have a right to presume, has
investigated the subject as laboriously as Sir
Oliver Lodge, what shall we think about it,
we bewildered men-in-the-street? And what
would we not give if we might put the judge
in a witness-box and hear him discourse upon
his years of experience?

One fact, to be sure, strikes us unmistakably
—that the anti-immortalists, like true human
beings, want to eat their cake and have it too.
No person is so unreasonable as the rationalist.
He will tell us that our psychic or spiritual
experiences are without value because we are
not scientists, not trained observers, not strict
thinkers, and often enough he is right; but
no sooner does an eminent scientist—Sir
William Crookes, for example, or Sir Oliver
Lodge—investigate " spiritualism " and pro-
nounce upon it in a sense which is opposed to
the prejudice of the sceptic, than he declares
that the investigator can no longer be truly
termed a scientist. I can only say that if I
were an anti-immortalist I should find Sir
Oliver's book about " Raymond " exceedingly
disconcerting. Had I comfortably settled myself into the conviction that after my death

I should be " nowhere and nothing," as Plato puts it, that book would make me shift about uneasily. How, I wonder, should I explain away the remarkable incident of the group-photograph?

Somebody, no doubt, has explained it away to his own satisfaction: but even if a physical explanation is manufacturable, it would not necessarily be true. And in feeling that the balance of probability tips over, almost decisively, in favour of Sir Oliver, I am probably at one with most of those who are not mental crustaceans. It is even possible that some day the perfervid rationalist, determined not to be convinced that he will survive death, may go through a humiliating diagnosis at the hands of the psycho-analyst.

If I am touching very lightly upon psychic research, it is because, in taking up a brief for the soul, I rely (as the lawyers have it) upon other considerations: but I feel, as most casual observers must, that the sceptic is often shallow, often hasty and often fanatical. He is fanatical when he refuses to admit that a message from the dead, transmitted by a medium, is evidence of survival because a living person is able to verify it. When that is so, the sceptic assures himself and the world that the medium extracted the message from the mind of the living person. Clearly, though, if no living person could verify it, the communicating spirit would be in the desperate state of a Long-lost Brother who has no scar by which he can be recognised. He is hasty when he performs a gleeful war-dance because a certain medium has been exposed. Ninety-nine grocers may put sand in their sugar, but there may still be one just grocer who does not. And he is shallow when he derides the evidence of spiritualism because communications from the dead are usually trivial and sometimes absurd. At the back of his mind he is still with Wordsworth, and assumes that immediately after death Aunt Sarah should become a glorious and omniscient being. We might just as well expect that an invalid, going to the sea, must in a single day become a Hercules of health. And if these messages have been trivial, what is the alternative? The Reverend Vale Owen provided many elevating discourses, but the sceptic can find no reason for attributing them to " the dead "; and Swedenborg's detailed account of heaven and hell makes no impression upon him. If you were telephoning to an acquaintance in Ohio, you would have the utmost difficulty in proving to him that you were yourself, provided that he were passionately determined not to believe it and, on the contrary, disputed every inch of the way. Your best chance of succeeding would be, in fact, to remind him of some trifle.

The battle is so fierce because the issue is so great; and the evidence for survival which has now been accumulated by psychic research would almost certainly satisfy the average man if it were evidence in favour of the unexciting proposition that there is vegetation on the moon.

IV

THE Hard-headed Man is of all men the most credulous, and, remembering his pedigree, we might pity him were he not so arrogant. For several generations his ancestors derided the ludicrous notion that the earth moves round the sun. It was so obvious that the sun moves round the earth: and any sensible man will believe the evidence of his own eyes. The Hard-headed Man now knows that his forerunners were mistaken. The less said about their mistake, the better for his self-respect. And, even more significantly, he knows also that they were deceived by their own position upon the moving earth.

When, however, he himself looks at a dead body, he too is content with the evidence of his own eyes. To him it is obvious that the intelligence which once informed that body is now, like the life that was in it, extinct. He has no patience with the ludicrous notion that a human being is a consciousness to which a temporary organism is attached rather than an organism which generates a temporary con-

F

sciousness: nor would it be possible to make him see that by looking at all things from the standpoint of a physical body he may be as much deceived as his ancestors were when they looked at the solar system as though the earth were its centre.

The truth may very well be that ever since we outgrew religion and took science for our director, we have been industriously putting the cart in front of the horse. No sooner did we apply ourselves, in the fifteenth century, to a study of physiology than we began to accumulate an assumption that we are primarily bodies. Medical students, playing catch with the heart of some person who was lately alive, slip easily into supposing that the invisible and intangible consciousness of that person was less real than the organ which they are merrily handling. They see, too, that a brain-lesion makes a man an imbecile and that a curried liver makes a colonel peppery. They soon learn, moreover, that drugs will change a man's behaviour, emotions and outlook upon life. And having observed these things, they straightway conceive that the soul (for I warned you that I should use that antique word) is merely a property of the body.

I see no difficulty in putting the horse in front of the cart. Up there, near the ceiling, is a bulb with a filament inside it. When I pressed the switch by the door, instantly the filament shone dazzlingly. One day, however, the bulb will refuse to work or someone, hitting it by accident, will break off a piece of the filament. I shall not then sit down in the darkness, lamenting that electricity exists no more. I shall get a new bulb from the shop round the corner; and the new bulb will show at once that the electricity was there all the time, waiting for the conditions which would enable it to reveal itself. So, too, when I look at a dead body, human, animal or vegetable, I see it as a broken or worn-out bulb, and suspect that the consciousness which once lighted it up has withdrawn into another state. In the same way, we ought probably to see the patients in a mental hospital as weak and damaged bulbs, incapable of manifesting the measure of consciousness which, normally, would rush into them. The medical student, in a word, cannot impress me by showing how simply he could destroy or admit the light of the soul by injuring or improving the body which it inhabits.

By this time, too, we ought, I suspect, to have learned that the universe is not a vast piece of mechanism, a tremendous clockwork toy. Perhaps, remembering the great effort of mind which our forefathers made when they unthought their supposition that the sun goes round the earth, we ought to make a comparable effort and try to think of the universe as an immense consciousness caught, imprisoned and broken up into millions of pieces by its impact with the atoms and electrical forces which exist in our familiar dimensions.

That hippopotamus in the ooze of an African stream; that bird-of-paradise dangling its incredibly beautiful tail as it sits on an Asian tree; that bounding dog with bright, mellow eyes; that bargee, spitting into the Thames; that ant-heap of little frantic men, howling themselves hoarse at a football match or an election; and the calm trees themselves, and all the goggle-eyed fishes in all the seas of the world, and the pebbles, the rocks, the seemingly-stationary hills and mountains, and the murderer, the judge and the saint—they are all physical traps in which consciousness is caught up, like thousands of pools and puddles which are left on a rock-pitted shore by an outgoing sea.

Once we have succeeded in looking at things in this heterodox way—seeing matter as an obstacle to mind, not mind as an attribute of matter—the change is so fundamental that every subject appears in an altered light and will probably seem a little more intelligible. To begin with, we realise that all through our lives we have been invisible, like a prince in a fairy-tale, and that everyone to whom we speak is really invisible. Their bodies are complicated, marvellous machines which they carry about with them, and in time they may lament, with W. B. Yeats,

" What shall I do with this absurdity—
  O heart, O troubled heart—this caricature,
  Decrepit age that has been tied to me
  As to a dog's tail? "

And if the machine gets out of order, its invisible owner may be so much affected by it that, instead of manifesting a magnificent or at least an intricate consciousness, he shrivels up into a mere querulous fragment of himself, all the best of him being driven down, under pressure of his ailing body, into the vast backward and abysm of the universal soul.

Now, as I am writing these words, though the illustration will probably seem so apt as to be suspect, across the landing death hovers about a small boy. How should I think of him: as the frail scrap of blurred consciousness which I last looked at, an hour ago, or as the vibrant, dancing scrap with which, a fortnight earlier, I was playing soldiers? That, I feel, was the true manifestation of his personality, not the listless ghost of a mind which is all that I can detect at present. The maladies of his body are obstructing the flow of life through it and, in consequence, driving inwards the consciousness which normally would float and glitter upon that vital stream.

We then perceive, too, that some brains and bodies are, as it were, semi-transparent (and, in this sense, even some faces), and that they can show much more of spiritual flame than the denser material can. Much of the consciousness which envelops all things could show itself through the person who was once named Plato: little indeed through the person who was once named Burke—the body-snatcher. In fact, if we see things from within outwards, history, anthropology, biology and the people about us all look so different that it might be worth our while to inspect them again. Moreover, this heliocentric point of view, if I may so call it, might form, as we shall see, the basis of the religion and morality which many people desire to find.

V

THE world has always great difficulty in changing its mental habits, and most men will never cease to think of themselves as physical bodies. To do so is natural, and yet may be mistaken. The opposite attitude, however, is not new. It has been widespread at certain times in India; it was widespread in Christendom when Christianity was most vital; and, working downward from the swift of mind to the slow, it may once more be generally, if vaguely, adopted. People, in the future, may once more think of themselves as being " souls ": for here is a view of man which we have merely lost, burying it under the mountain of physical facts which men have discovered since the end of the Middle Ages.

When I think of our present state I find myself remembering a Sunday afternoon when, as a very little boy, I was looking at a book of pictures that represented various benighted races. Among them was a picture of Hindus prostrating themselves in front of the car of the god Juggernaut. The missionary who had written the book informed his readers that "these unhappy creatures, blinded by superstition, willingly allow the wheels of the huge car to crush them to death. Be thankful, therefore," he concluded, "that you were born in a Christian land." We, too, however, have our idol, our Juggernaut (they spell it differently to-day), and the massed feeling of our age demands that we should worship it. Science does not kill its devotees, but it paralyses them. One of the secrets of modern unhappiness, although nobody acknowledges it, is that, under the domination of the scientific spirit, we continuously suppress every part of our minds except the intellectual part. The rest is in danger of atrophy: and the psychoanalysts have shown how large the rest of it is. We dare not indulge in even a little of the free speculation and the emotional thinking which are natural to men. In a word, we dare not use the deeper layers of consciousness; and if, for example, we experience a mystical sense of God, either in a beautiful solitude or a noisy thoroughfare, we hide it away, remembering our scientific pundits, just as a boy will guiltily conceal from a schoolmaster some irrelevant sketch done in a happy day-dream.

Why was it, though, that (about twenty-five years ago) Bergson's philosophy became of a sudden not only popular but even fashionable?

Despite the vigour and clarity of his thought and style, that philosophy is not so elementary that we should expect the general reader to adopt *Creative Evolution* as his bedside-book, his metaphysical nightcap. The explanation is obviously that the world of intelligent readers experienced a strange delight and relief when a first-class thinker, using the tool of intellect, gave them reason for doubting whether intellect is more than a specialised function of the mind and one which, like a microscope, has no more than a limited use. Men wanted to breathe more deeply than the strait-waistcoat of science permitted. They wanted to let their minds range beyond the narrow boundaries of attested fact. Bergson's work is not now studied as it once was, but that is only because most people will give their attention to nothing but " the latest thing." In ten years' time a new work by Sir James Jeans may cause as little excitement as " creative evolution " or psycho-analysis to-day. In fact, so complete is the slavery of the modern man to mere intellectual fashion that he is capable of allowing the contents of his mind to depend upon the ingenuity of a publisher's advertisement. We still want more freedom than science can grant at present, for a man is no more wholly scientific than wholly æsthetic. Indeed, I wonder if the foremost scientists of the age—they who are the custodians of human thought, they upon whom, in a descending multitude, most of us depend for our philosophical judgments—may not, like humorous kings, be secretly embarrassed by our extreme veneration, doubting whether they have better means than the simple man of actually deciding, on behalf of their generation, whether there is any God and whether a man has any soul. In public, all scientists must necessarily cease to be human, for science would have no value if it were not the intellectual currency of mankind; but in private many a scientist may dally with shamelessly unscientific notions.

Reason is like gold, a convenient medium of exchange. When, in the seventh century before Christ, men began to adopt a gold currency they must have been delighted by its convenience; and they never went back to the system of barter. In much the same way they discovered in Athens, and re-discovered in Italy, that the minds of men have no common factor except the observations of the senses and the deductions of reason. Our intellects vary in strength but, unless they are damaged, not in kind. If you say that you are in love, another man may reply that he does not believe it, but if you assert that elm-trees never bear grapes, he is unlikely to begin a dispute. The satisfaction of discovering a medium of mental exchange was so great that we have ceased ever since to barter our private, spiritual, emotional, intuitional goods; and now we have drifted into the assumption that no goods can be worth anything unless intellect is able to put a price upon them.

We may revolt against this worship of observation and deduction, and yet recognise that, in various kinds of work, these are the best tools. No one wishes to be treated by a doctor who merely guesses (though many of us are) or by a doctor who works upon the mediæval system whereby, for example, walnuts were prescribed as a stimulant to the brain because a walnut and a brain have a rough likeness in appearance: and yet, even in medicine, we may hope more of a doctor who adds intuition to text-book knowledge.

Bergson boldly challenged this worship of intellect, affirming that we are incapable of seizing truth if we use only one of our faculties. The man of common sense will suspect that he is right. Our specialists in intellectual gymnastics perform the most prodigious feats. They have classified all the forms which we find in our world. They can weigh a sun. They have discovered (or so they believe at the moment) that space is curved. Or listen to this extract, given by *The Times*, of a lecture by Sir James Jeans:

" If we wished to maintain stellar ages of millions of millions of years, the only possible course was to suppose that observation and theory were wholly illusory and that astronomers and mathematicians had both been exploring a complete mare's nest. As regarded theory, that supposition was, Sir James Jeans said, not wholly preposterous. If appearances were not wholly illusory, the whole evolution of the universe must have occurred far more rapidly than had usually been supposed.

" In conclusion, Sir James Jeans discussed what he called the risky and highly speculative, but absorbingly interesting arguments by which Sir Arthur Eddington had attempted to evaluate the cosmical constant which fixed the inherent curvature of space. Einstein and De Sitter had recently said that there was not a scrap of observational evidence to support the existence of that constant. But the investigations in regard to it were noteworthy, because they for the first time in the history of science brought the largest and the smallest objects in the universe into direct and intimate relationship. In such ways as this science was just entering on its latest and most comprehensive problem —namely, the study of the whole universe as a single entity. The first tentative results had proved very surprising, and indeed for the man of science disconcerting. They illustrated once again that it was usually the totally unexpected that happened in science. The unaided human mind could seldom penetrate far into the darkness which lay beyond the circle of light formed by direct observational knowledge, yet perhaps many would feel that the nature of the results obtained was less surprising than the fact that it was possible to obtain results at all."

The reflective man will certainly be impressed by these immensities of time and space, but he is likely to be more impressed by the fact that an almost invisible speck, who goes by the name of Sir Arthur Eddington, should be able to examine the universe so intrepidly. David was more remarkable even than Goliath. We shall wonder, in fact, which is the more astonishing, matter or the mind which assays it; and we may return from our astronomical odyssey with a suspicion that the physical universe is wholly irrelevant to any part of us except our bodies. It must have been from such a standpoint that the Indian hermit said to Edward Carpenter, " I do not care whether the sun goes round the earth or the earth round the sun," and that Emerson wrote

> " A ruddy drop of manly blood
>   The surging sea outweighs."

At least we ought not, in our vulgar way, to abase ourselves before the universe because it is large. If size is to cow us, then a New York skyscraper should be sufficient. The mind is immeasurable, and once we have realised that it is neither large nor small, we can go to bed unscared by the vast bogey of the physical universe. No white-hot sun, we may suppose, has ever experienced the ecstasy of which the mystics, from Jalálu-'d-dín Rúmi to Jacob Boehme, have spoken; and it may be that only upon this insignificant earth has any spiritual history been made.

Our muscles are at their strongest and most elastic when we are in the twenties. Then it is that our brains also are at their best: then that we can argue with an ingenuity and a brilliance which we subsequently lose. The world, we might therefore think, should submit itself to the rule of the twenty-year-olds, but the world has never done so, because in the conduct of real life insight, foresight and experience are of more importance than nimbleness of intelligence. The intellect works in patterns. It is, like the bee, a natural geometriser; and only symmetry can content it. For all that we know, the axiom that two and two make four may be palpably absurd to the mind of an archangel. And just as a man is all intellect (if he has any) at twenty but will dote less upon a syllogism when he has had some taste of real life, so is Western humanity at present in its twenties and relying upon intellect, as a young man does, to solve mysteries for which intellect alone is as ill-adapted as a pair of scales would be for the weighing of beauty.

VI

IT is so long since the science-worshipper considered religion seriously that when he brings himself to do so he acts like a professor who, being asked if he plays bridge, remembers that long ago he did play whist. He assumes, for instance, that life and the soul are one and the same—as indeed they were thought to be by a good many savage tribes and are still thought to be by many theologians: and no doubt he would remind us that the word "pneuma" meant both "spirit" and "breath." Some day, perhaps, a chemist, combining certain properties, will produce (instead of reproducing) "life"; but it is more than unlikely that he will have put together a "soul." We have no cause for supposing that life and consciousness are identical; and most of our scepticism concerning the soul is due simply to this ancient confusion. The evidence of psychic research, if we accept it, powerfully suggests that life and consciousness have no more intimate connection than a river and the boat that glides upon it. If "Raymond's" personality can exist when the life in his body has gone out, we must admit that his life and his personality were distinct the one from the other.

Suppose, on the contrary, that we think of a great sea of consciousness breaking for ever against the substance of the physical universe, we shall then look upon the evolution of forms as a result of that great sea for ever striving to force its way through the obstacles of our three dimensions; gradually getting through it and, in the course of so doing, continually forcing matter to take finer and finer forms in order that more and more of consciousness may flow through.

Mere life itself has a thoroughly bad record. In fact, we might say that, in respect of this world at least, it plays the part which the mediæval Christians and the ancient Persians attributed to the Devil. No sooner does life arise within a fragment of matter than it shows a ferocious determination not to let go. All that it wants, and wants with the utmost vehemence, is to save itself from extinction: with the result that Nature, by which we mean the life-principle, has no moral sense, no fellow-feeling, no mercy and no justice, but, quite contrariwise, maintains itself by that abominable system whereby no scrap of life can persist except by eating up some other scrap. Here, then, we may see why every man is afraid of death and yet also feels that his fear is at least unworthy. It is the life in him that dreads death, acting as instinctively as the eyelid which closes when any object approaches it; and it is the soul in him that scorns this instinct. I suspect, indeed, that no man is any more able to conceive of his consciousness going out altogether than he can conceive of unoccupied Space. He is muddled because, though his soul knows that it cannot expire, his life knows that it must: and the life in most men is stronger than the soul.

Now, it looks as though for an immense period of the world's pre-history hardly a trickle of spirit made its way through matter; as though the rage of life was all that the world could show for perhaps a million years. Think of a brontosaurus, a mammoth, a tiger and a flea, and you perceive at once that they are all the abject slaves of " the life-force." In fact, if a selfless impulse could arise within a flea, it would probably explode his little mechanism. And then conceive how gradually a sense of fellow-feeling silted into the world. How did it begin to make its way? Some people might tell us that it began in the mother-animal's instinct to protect the life of her offspring from the father-animal's instinct to gobble it up; and others might tell us that certain insects and animals refrained from killing their kind because they felt or learned that there is safety in numbers. It does not matter at all how life was forced, or (as it were) beguiled, into letting a little selflessness come through. What does matter is that in course of time it did come through; and that fellow-feeling grew into love, and that love proceeded to rebel against the edicts of life; until at last the earth achieved a few men and women—and some dogs, too,—who disregarded the tremendous instinct of self-preservation which is perhaps the one and only characteristic of life, and thought less of their own safety or continuity than of the welfare of other creatures. Even now most men and women are little more than Nature's automata, driven onward solely by the raw passion that is in life. There are monsters without conscience or sympathy who, because of their physical appearance, are considered to be men. Moreover, these ingenious, tricky little brains in which we human beings have specialised are as fecund a source of trouble in the world as life itself is. They enable life to be a thousand times more cunning than its own plain instinct could ever make it. The little scrap of spiritual force within us has now, indeed, a hard time, assailed on the one side by the selfishness of life and on the other by the resourcefulness of intelligence. From the first we derive our cruelty, from the second our craftiness—the two chief blots upon human nature, the two characteristics of man which prevent the earth from becoming, at least for men and women, an earthly paradise.

VII

I REMEMBER to have read long ago, and not without surprise, how Mr. Gladstone himself suggested that immortality is not the birthright of every human being, but that people, or some people, become immortal gradually. At least it is necessary, in order to apprehend the point of view which I am describing, that we should conceive that the life and the spirit in a man are separate and only temporary partners. As you read these words you test them with your intelligence and also, perhaps, with another part of your nature —the part which knows whether a thought rings true upon it or not; and all the while your heart, your bowels, your tissues, are doing their appointed work on behalf of the life which is in you, and you are unconscious of their operations. It is just as though the life in you, pursuing its own ends, were a rudimentary creature to which you are strangely allied. This has now become a " hard saying " to most occidentals and, no doubt, to many orientals too: but it comes from a point of view which is implicit in numerous utterances of Jesus, and was implicit, consequently, in the mind of the Middle Ages. It is even more definitely contained in the philosophy of Buddhism. One of the first practices in spiritual training which a Buddhist monk attempts is precisely this realisation that his bodily life is, as it were, outside him; for a Buddhist monk is instructed (as one himself told me) to think, as he walks through the village with his begging-bowl, " A leg is moving forward, a knee is bending, a head is feeling the air upon it, a hand is proffering a bowl, a tongue is speaking." And when Tennyson induced in himself an uncanny but exciting sensation by repeating his own name (and many people might share his experience if they would), he must have achieved something of the realisation at which the Buddhist monk is aiming—the realisation that he, essentially, was not the nineteenth-century bundle of chemicals, vitality and intelligence which went through the world as Alfred Tennyson.

If the life in us, then, is no more our true and essential self than the body which it defends and sustains with a skill so ancient and so marvellous, what attributes of our complete being may pertain to the spirit, to the part of us which, according to the spiritualists and to millions of other persons, will not become extinct when the life fades from our bodies? Even intelligence, as it now is, cannot be an attribute of spirit: for we develop an intelligence which is of use to us in coping with the particular conditions of life in this world. Our minds, we could say, are reflections of the world in which we find ourselves. In a different world—say, in Mars or the Moon—we should have developed quite different talents and interests because the conditions would be quite different.

We ought, then, to realise that the spirit is something which does not manifest itself all day or even every day, except in the saint. During most of our lives it is latent. We have agreed that the world is crammed with scoundrels and dummies: dummies who prattle idly in the lounges of seaside hotels or boarding-houses, and elsewhere too, scoundrels who direct their energy and intelligence against the lives, the fortunes or the happiness of others: we have seen how difficult it is to suppose that such beings are immortal spirits. We should not be dismayed by this difficulty if we could clear our minds of the old supposition about Aunt Sarah—that the entire personality, except its physical body, is immortal; and the notion that people are continuously in touch with the immortal principle within them.

The immortal principle, I suggest, is active and visible only when a man acts in opposition to the selfish instincts of the life in his body. We see it, that is to say, whenever he forgets himself and does something out of love for another creature. Every time that he has a brotherly feeling, a desire to help, an impulse of true love, the immortal bit in him grows. Sometimes he will have no opportunity, or will not take any, of revealing it again for months or years: but it is there—in the deeps. And that may be the whole secret of progress and civilisation. Men become more and more ready to sacrifice themselves or their interests for others. The immortal bit becomes, in this way, more and more accessible, so that in a genuinely civilised society we find an increasing number of men and women in whom there is so much general goodwill that we could rely upon them to act nobly if ever the occasion arose. Once we have put something into the spiritual bank, it remains there for ever as capital which is earning compound interest. The worst scoundrel who ever lived may have had a moment of kindness towards a cat or a dog, and for that one moment he was acting as an immortal spirit. The dummies, too, though physically repulsive and intellectually tedious, may at a pinch reveal surprising resources of sympathy and love. Indeed, we may apprehend what the Syrian mystic meant when he said that " God is love " if we perceive that love does not spring from the life-force or the intelligence of a man, and is, on the contrary, against Nature—supernatural—and may even strike across the grain of the three-dimensional universe because it comes from an entirely different region. Sympathy and love, the signals of spirituality, the manifestations of the immortal, arise in us when we recognise that only physically are we and other creatures completely isolated. Life makes for separation; love, for unity. In consequence, when we have realised the fundamental unity of all things, we perceive that whenever we fight for our puny personal selves we are throwing away a chance of becoming greater in consciousness. The whole world agrees that if any man may be called spiritual it is such a man as Saint Francis of Assisi, and we admit his spirituality because he acted as though other people—and birds and animals and the moon and the sun—were as real to him as his own particular self. His consciousness was, as it were, almost as much inside other creatures as it was inside his own body.

If we take this point of view, we shall not be surprised that few people behave in a manner becoming to immortal and spiritual beings: for the unscrupulous financier is using only the intelligence which the life-force within him has developed, and the girl on the table at Rouen was a representative of crude life alone. When we thus divide our emotions into those which come from life-instincts and those which come from love-impulses, we are really making the distinction of " body " and " spirit " that so enrages the man who, in the fashion of our time, imagines that he has shattered a philosophy whenever he shouts the word " dualism "; but this very dualism will at least show us in a flash why religion and sex have always been the two great driving-forces in humanity, and why they have often pulled strenuously against each other.

The sex-impulse in itself—that is to say, as it is common to men, animals, birds, fishes, insects and even the vegetable world—is a manifestation of life, an urgent desire on the part of life to reproduce itself and so to avoid extinction. Buddhism and Christianity, however, counselled men to think little of their lives and to think much of aiding the sick, the unhappy and the unwise; in other words, to expand beyond themselves, beyond the personal interests which are so dear to the life in us. These two religions, therefore, tried to evoke the small, submerged, slowly-growing immortal principle within men; bade them suppress their life-instincts and develop their love-impulses; and the immense influence of Buddhism and Christianity may be due to the fact that spirit, once it has effected a rift in matter and life, can never be driven out again. Each of these religions has done much to spiritualise humanity: and spiritualisation is the only true civilisation, for our measure of civilisation depends not upon labour-saving or body-killing devices, but upon the extent to which our society has developed fellow-feeling: and if neither Buddhism nor Christianity has had more than a partial success, that is because life came raging into the world a good million years before spirit, striking down perhaps from another dimension, could even make itself faintly felt.

VIII

SEEN from this angle the history of human ideas and human deeds is much less depressing than it seemed at first. When we learn from *The Golden Bough* and other books that men based their earliest religious conceptions upon blunders of observation and deduction, and that they steadily refined those conceptions but would not wholly cast them away, we can say, with the orthodox twentieth-century man, that all these later religious ideas are negligible because they began in error, and that ingenious apologists, like Plutarch, were desperately trying to save ideas which were destined to collapse when Intelligence became adult: or we can say that these ideas derive from a spiritual world with which, for many thousands of years, men had only a connection of the most tenuous kind; that these ideas continued persistently to play upon the mind of man and were distorted for a long time by his growing but inadequate intelligence, until in the end he cultivated intellect to so high a point that he trusted more to that specialised function of the brain than to the profound intimations of a spiritual world which had always haunted humanity, and so inaugurated an age of dry rationalism. In other words, we can see religion as an elaborate structure built upon a marsh of ignorant fancy, or as a light, coming from a great depth of consciousness and slowly spreading through a tangled forest not only of mistaken notions, but also, in these days, of accurate notions about the physical universe and the physical forms of men and women.

Anyone who takes the latter view will find that historians never write the history which he would most like to read. I always wish that they would explain how it is that men seem suddenly, in a book of history, to have tastes and sensibilities and moral standards which the men of the previous generation did not possess and might have despised. The happy professor who feels that he can explain everything in terms either of economics or of climate should be able at once to give us an answer; but he and his colleagues would not agree with one another, and they would have a further quarrel with the psycho-analyst who would offer us a different and an equally " brilliant " explanation. Why did men cease to demand the pleasure of the amphitheatre? How did they outgrow the world-old assumption that slavery was as natural as eating? What caused them to abandon cannibalism? Why is it that at present only a half of society can see that stag-hunting is an anachronism, or that it is obviously more civilised to eat fruit and vegetables than the flesh and the organs of animals? These questions—these that touch upon the development of man as a spiritual being—are seemingly of no interest to the university-minded historian. He will state, indeed, that war and politics are the pair of refractory horses which a historian has to drive.

To some of us laymen it looks as though a struggling spirit in man had gradually forced its way through a thicket of habit and inertia; as though, every now and again, a man is born who has a finer sense of true civilisation than that of his contemporaries, and that if he comes too early (like Wycliffe), he remains a voice in the wilderness—and a voice that history may never " record " for us—but that sometimes his contemporaries are ripe to respond. Even now there may be men and women among us who belong spiritually to the twenty-first century, just as Leonardo da Vinci and Sir Thomas More were obviously ahead of the fifteenth century by some hundreds of years. At least it is plain that in every age there must have been certain men who were the best men alive. The best? When I use that word I mean, once again, men in whom sympathy and love were more highly developed than in the men about them: for the history of intellectual ability would make a curve across the chart of history quite at variance with the curve made by moral beauty. That is a distinction which Jesus, who so often exalted the simplicity of children, must have had constantly in mind.

I lack the scholarship which a man would need if he were to write a spiritual history of humanity, but I think he would find that moral beauty has burned up so intermittently that its course, if traced on a map of the world, would be as erratic as a firefly's. I see, too, that he would have much difficulty in separating spirituality (or the manifestations of sympathy and love) from intellectual progress, and again from the moral prepossessions of our time. I suspect that he would see that for an immense period there was more spirituality in Egypt than in any other part of the world; that the leadership of humanity then passed to India, and that love was growing among the ancient Hindus while the Babylonians and Assyrians were achieving merely a material advance. I suspect also that he would recognise the sixth century before Christ as perhaps the greatest in the whole of our history: for it was then that Confucius bequeathed a high moral code to millions of human beings; then that the tender spirit of Lâo-tsze counselled men " not to act from any personal motive, to conduct affairs without feeling the trouble of them, to taste without being aware of the flavour, to account the great as small and the small as great, to recompense injury with kindness "; and then also that, several thousands of miles away, Gautama gave forth his sad and magnificent philosophy of which the very core is the doctrine that the ego is an illusion, and egoism, in consequence, the root of all the sorrow in the world. And from that age he would probably pass to ancient Athens, disregarding the stupendous intellectual achievement of Aristotle and concentrating our attention upon the spiritual perceptions of Plato—perhaps the most completely developed personality who has ever lived in this world, a man in whom intellect and intuition were equally powerful. And next? He would probably pass from the spiritual heroism of the great Roman stoics to the world-changing influence of the Galilæan: that beautiful spirit whose perception that only pity, love and a sense of unity had any importance for humanity was destined to spread so strangely across the Western world, just as the similar perceptions of Gautama had spread through so great a part of the East. The adoption of Christianity as the religious ideal of the West is the most dramatic spiritual change of which we have any record. It is comparable, indeed, with the changing of a chrysalis into a butterfly; and during the Dark Ages that followed the collapse of Roman ideas, it was the Christian ideal that saved our hemisphere from spiritual extinction. Again and again, until it was strangled by intellectuality, as a tree may be strangled by ivy, that spirit of unity and selflessness revealed itself brilliantly; but the spiritual historian would find, I surmise, that even before the Crusades his trail led him away from Europe and into Islam, and would see that spirituality was not then so bright a flame in any part of Europe as it was among the Sufis—as it was, perhaps, in Hallāj, who was martyred for saying "I am the Truth," and whose nature can be divined from the words "We are sundered from God by two steps only: one step out of this world, one step out of the next world, and lo, you are there with the Lord!"

And then our historian might discover that intellectuality began, and steadily continued, to side-track humanity; that men became more and more enthralled by their exploration of the physical universe and by their mastery of natural forces; and that the saint, or the man of love, had been displaced as an ideal by the scientist, or the man of knowledge. And yet he would still find that love was at work in the world. He would find traces of it, at a certain period, in the Quakers, despite their rigid judgments of right and wrong. He would find it, too, in the gradual recognition, during the eighteenth century, that slavery was inhumane and that sailors, criminals and idiots ought not to be treated with an Assyrian brutality.

And we, as we read that unwritten history, would perceive that, in spite of the incalculable evil which men have done, there have been, over and over again, manifestations of a spirit in man which is so beautiful in its abnegation of self that, after all, we should not despair of mankind. We should find, too, that the really great persons in our history are not those who catch the limelight of orthodox historians. Asoka would seem more important than Attila; Epictetus than Julius Cæsar; John Wesley than Robert Walpole; and Father Damien than Bismarck. We might even discern that there is more spirituality in many a dog than there was in Napoleon Bonaparte.

IX

AT one time or another everyone of nimble intelligence has alighted upon the notion that no act is unselfish because a so-called unselfish act gives pleasure to an unselfish nature. The man who makes this antique discovery is usually so much excited by it that he cannot listen to any reply. The truth is that he has been tricked by mere words. The exceptional person who actually finds his happiness in doing good to another is merely a person who has no self, no greedy and clamorous ego; and to call his disposition selfish is as ludicrous as to say that a yacht with the wind behind her is in competition with those who are tacking against it; or, to put the matter in another way, the man who is instinctively unselfish has reversed the engines of Nature. We become confused only because we apply the same word—pleasure —to the self-gratification of Napoleon Bonaparte and the selfless love-expression of Father Damien.

Love, then, is the supernatural element in a man; and wherever we see love manifested we are in the presence of the soul. Perhaps we never understand the significance of many among the sayings of Jesus until we have seized the idea that love is—to phrase it very crudely —a foreigner in the physical universe, a " white radiance " from heaven that shines through the " dome of many-coloured glass " which is our earth-bound existence, a force from another dimension which disturbs the normal arrangement of a three-dimensional state. And conceiving it as a " white radiance," we can understand at once that it hardly ever comes through into a man's personality without refraction. Emperors, diplomatists, generals, and men of " big business " have merely modified the machinery of human life, making our external conditions more comfortable or, as a rule, more painful. The men who have made our real history, who have altered the feelings of men toward each other and toward " the lower creations," are the founders of great religions and the best of their followers.

In Jesus and Gautama the " white radiance " came through with hardly a stain, if any : and that is precisely why most men would name them as the two highest representatives of humanity. We could not expect so much of their followers, nor do we find it. The early Quakers, for example, did try to regard every man as a brother, every woman as a sister : but they limited their sympathy by enclosing it within a narrow code of right and wrong. In the same way, the early Puritans wished passionately to see men discipline the crude instincts of life and nature, and behave with a dignity befitting souls that had been created by God: but we all know how closely they came to resemble the Pharisees of an earlier age and how severely they would have reprimanded Jesus for plucking an ear of corn on the Sabbath or turning the water into wine. And so it has always been—high-intentioned men continually adulterating their love-impulses by mixing them with moral or theological ideas which were merely of their time. There is, I suppose, no more horrible illustration of this tendency than the grim and fantastic handiwork of the Inquisition or the nightmarish influence of Calvin's grotesque theology.

If, again, we conceive of the soul as something which is not completely separated from all other souls, as a body is from all other bodies, we shall understand a number of puzzling facts. We shall understand, for instance, why telepathy is possible, and why intuition, or an immediate perception of another person's state of mind, is a faculty which can be consciously developed. I know a certain man who at a dinner-party will sometimes astonish his neighbour by describing the house in which she was brought up and the number, appearances and dispositions of her early companions. He says that he " takes a dive out of his own mind and comes up, on the other side, in the mind of the person to whom he is speaking " : but this would be possible only to a considerably de-egotised nature. He says, too, that he developed his intuition by trusting to it, riskily at first, but afterwards with confidence.

On a much bigger scale we shall understand also why all the great mystics have been inspired by one longing and why they all bring back the same report of their spiritual experience. They report that it is possible, when the senses and the monkey-like personal thoughts have been stilled, to pass through the ensuing darkness and to wake up, interiorly, in a state which they compare with light. Christian, Sufi, Buddhist, Brahmanist: Lâo-tsze, Plotinus, Jalálu-'d-dín Rúmi, Saint Teresa, Boehme, Eckhardt, Vivekananda: they all agree that " ecstasy " is a result of sending the ego to sleep so that it shall no longer obstruct the One Consciousness which envelops the fifty thousand million separated objects that compose the universe. And the hunger which inspired them, one and all, was to lose themselves in that underlying Oneness.

We may therefore be wise if we abandon the antiquated notion that each soul, like Huxley's atom, is a hard little separate thing which will never lose its present identity: and if, on the contrary, we think of it as something that is for ever striving to overflow into others—to " lose his life " in order that he may " find it." That is, at least, precisely the effect of sympathy and love. How far, we may well wonder, can the soul extend its boundaries? The answer is, according to the great mystics, that it can do so indefinitely, until it could not accurately be termed a separate soul at all. That last ecstasy is, in the lovely phrase of Plotinus, " the flight of the Alone to the Alone "; but obviously the return of a separate soul into the universal soul, taking place at an immeasurable distance from the mental level upon which we normally live, is an experience of extreme rarity.

Nobody could be better aware than I that these pages have given an indication of what the soul is that will convince or satisfy few people. To the hard-headed or the matter-of-fact I shall seem to be playing with a nebulous pseudo-mysticism; but they should pause to ask themselves if they are not demanding that the soul should be demonstrated as though it were a visible object under a microscope, and they should explain the presence in the world of those unnatural factors, sympathy and love. I have suggested, then, that these are the earthly intimations of the soul: that the soul is not separate from the "communion of souls": that it expands inwards indefinitely, showing, like a cube that begins to pierce a plane, only a tip of itself when once it has become involved in a body and in our three-dimensional world; and that it is not native to our time and space, but "cometh from afar." And if it does not belong to time and space (for which reason, perhaps, the soul may feel ageless when the body has become a sorry caricature of what it once was), then it is not born when life enters a body and does not die when the life in the body goes out. It is, rather, captured by the life in a body and subsequently released unwillingly.

The sense of an underlying unity, which is, in this view, characteristic of the soul and which the great mystics have always proclaimed, may assume foolish or distorted forms when it begins to involve itself in the life-stream of the body or the thought-stream of the brain. The final ecstasy, for example, is not a state which anyone should try to induce in himself. It should be left to come when it must. Those who try to experience it prematurely manifest, as a rule, nothing but an emptiness of mind which is not far removed from imbecility. Those, again, who seize the principle that we should love all men, frequently end up as ineffective believers in " the ultimate amiability of all things." Again, there are people who catch a glimpse of that fundamental unity in which every soul has its base, and who obfuscate it with the sexuality which arises within them from the operation of mere life. Shelley attempted to apply his doctrine of universal love to sexual expression: and an even clearer example is to hand in Walt Whitman. They mistook their way because they did not recognise that souls are not completely separate, but that bodies are, and that an expression which is natural to the soul cannot be fittingly used by the body. A similar misapplication of the sense of unity is common among people who are developing spiritually, and accounts for the wreck of innumerable spiritual communities. In fact, it is true that the man who is becoming spiritual is also especially likely to become more sexual than he had been hitherto, so difficult is it for some people to distinguish between soul-impulses and life-instincts.

In our own time we have seen another remarkable manifestation of that sense of unity which comes from the spiritual principle in man. As religion declined, men tended more and more to advocate socialism and communism. These men would rebut with vigour and scorn the suggestion that they do so because there is something immortal within them, but the suggestion, nevertheless, may hit the target. If it is true, then we are seeing once again an attempt to apply to "earthly" affairs a condition that is normal in "heaven." Communism is unquestionably the ideal state; but sympathy and love have at present made so little headway against the huge forces of life, intelligence and egoism, that to advocate communism now is like leaving a cannibal to operate a power-station.

Is it not possible, though, to say something more definite about the long-lost soul of man? I do not think it is, unless we call the evidence of bygone mystics and of modern clairvoyants and psychical researchers. The earlier mystics have not been able to check the great landslide toward scepticism. The clairvoyants and the psychical researchers are, to most persons, witnesses of doubtful value. If, however, we relied upon what they say, we should learn that after death the personality of a man does not, like Aunt Sarah, suddenly change out of recognition. Indeed, it seems to continue for some time with little alteration, existing among replicas of earthly objects or, if Plato was right, among the models of which earthly objects are grosser representations. We gather, too, that the soul withdraws farther and farther from the life which it has left, losing touch with our conditions and our interests precisely as a friend who goes to live in California will be less and less able to "follow" the references in our letters to private events in London. Again, from all the evidence that exists, I should say that one thing is clear—namely, that the more a soul has manifested sympathy and love while it was "alive," the less strange and ill-at-ease will it find itself when it is "dead." Nor, if I dare venture a guess, ought we to expect, in the old way, that we shall wake up in bliss. The pain of a last illness will doubtless be over and gone, but paradise itself could not make us happy unless we have rid ourselves of inward discord. If we cannot be happy where we are, we are not likely to become happy by going to the other side of the world or to that psychic land east of the sun, west of the moon.

X

I SHALL make no idle attempt to prove that God exists. What would this really involve? An absurd attempt to satisfy the exigent little human intellect that within and about the visible universe there is an all-including consciousness. If this were a fact, how could there possibly be evidence for it that would be satisfactory to science? Why, to begin with, if God exists, he, she or it would obviously be as incomprehensible to the mind of a man as the contents of Newton's mind were incomprehensible to the maggot in the apple which he observed with such remarkable consequences. Consider merely that we cannot imagine even a million miles or, for that matter, a thousand. To our infantile imaginations a million and a thousand miles are the same: they are just a very long distance, a feeble multiplication of the longest distance over which our eyes have looked. Obviously, then, it is quite impossible to catch even a glimpse, with the mind's eye, of a consciousness which is aware of every single object, sensation and movement in the whole of space and time, past, present and future: and that is what we must mean by " God."

One point, however, seems clear to most of us: that God could be no more like a man than like a leaf, a microbe, a wind, a killer-whale, an electron, a sun or a nebula. We are therefore a long way from the happy time when our remote ancestors fancied that by threats or prayers they could induce God to increase their crops, to provide rain because they wanted it, or to make the sun stand still: and when I read that " the churches are praying for rain," I always picture the bishops and minor priests as coal-black figures attired only in loin-cloths and nose-rings. The reader may remember how that grim woman Mrs. Ruskin (the mother) once asked a young girl, " Do you love God? "; how the girl dutifully answered, " Yes "; and how Mrs. Ruskin retorted crushingly, " Nobody can love God. It is impossible for us even to imagine Him." And in illustration of that impossibility the reader may also recall how a faint-hearted follower once asked for moral support from a leader of the suffragettes; and how this leader replied, " Pray to God, dear. She will help you." No doubt, the scientists are justified in stating that the earth is ninety-three million miles away from the sun, and that the electrons in an atom are grouped round a nucleus: but to satisfy a world-made intellect that the universe exists within the consciousness of a single being is as impossible as it would be to prove to a ladybird in a library that the shelves contain records of human thought and emotion during two or three thousand years.

The ladybird would realise only that she was travelling over a variety of surfaces—the spines of the books: and those gallant scientists who try to get some impression of " God " by considering the apparatus of the universe are probably in much the same position as the ladybird. They have demonstrated nothing but that the universe is apparently a slave to certain laws or habits: that, for example, there are no triangular suns. To think of the universe as being, therefore, only a senseless machine may be as superficial as to suppose that all the motor-cars on Broadway do really propel themselves and could have come into existence without the initial work of a human intelligence. Once they are made, they cannot change into carrots or fairies. They can do much, but they cannot (at present) swim or fly. In the same way, the bodies in the universe seem, fortunately for us, to have limited possibilities. They remain poised where they are, and going round and round or onward and onward. So again, in our little pea of a world, the fig tree continually manifests its " dharma " (or appointed course), and does not disconcertingly bear thistles.

We are still so anthropomorphic that although we have sponged out our early impression of God as a benevolent patriarch, we tend to assume that these habits of the universe were imposed upon it by a consciousness not wholly unlike our own. This could only be true in the sense that a man and a ladybird resemble each other in one respect—that each has a feeling that he or she exists. If God exists, he (she or it) must contain all possible kinds of consciousness, and therefore among them the kind which we ourselves possess. If this were true, we might understand that prayer, after all, may be effective within certain limits. The modern man assumes, I suppose, that prayer was merely a way of drawing strength from our own subconscious forces: but who knows how far that subconscious base of the human mind may extend? For all that we do know about it, the subconscious mind may become, at a great depth, a huge reservoir from which all human beings draw in common. Or we could say that the whole of human consciousness may be like the trunk of a tree; national and racial consciousness like the major boughs; and all our sharply-separated selves, our obstreperous egos, like twigs, none of them recognising its kinship with any other. Looking at ourselves in this way, we might even understand the secret of Christian Science and faith-healing; for no genuine " agnostic " will assert that there is no truth in the claims of Christian Science, or feel confident that " auto-suggestion," in the orthodox meaning of the word, is the only possible explanation of its successes. We must remember, however, that if most of the soul is normally submerged, a great part of our life-instinct is in the same condition. There is, in the " subconscious," both a tiger and an angel; and in " crowd-emotion " we may see either the one or the other. It is the hidden angel within us that a beautiful religious ceremony evokes. It is the hidden tiger which is awakened during a panic or by the agitator who appeals to the egoism in his audience.

Remembering that the part of " God's " allconsciousness which humanity or any single human being can touch is only one aspect of it, we shall see that God cannot, for our benefit, change laws which a non-human part of his consciousness devised, but that, nevertheless, he might still be an inexhaustible reservoir of all those forces of will and emotion which can be of use to men. And retaining in our thoughts this image of the tree, we may get some notion of what it is that happens to a mystic in ecstasy.

The twig-consciousness expands along the branch, then along the main bough, then down the trunk of the tree, and finally, flowing into the very roots, may experience a direct association with the soil of God's consciousness from which the whole tree derives its being.

There are only three ways of solving the question of God's existence. We may deny that he exists, though we shall probably do so only if we imagine him grotesquely; we can take the sentimental view that he is personal and benevolent, and that evil and pain are insoluble mysteries; or we can say that he exists because he must, but that he is necessarily unimaginable and incomprehensible. The "problem of evil" is an insurmountable stumbling-block to any theologian, for it is obviously impossible to reconcile the fact that "nature" is based upon atrocious suffering with the conception of a Creator who is wiser and tenderer than the best of men. God, as the atheists were wont to declare triumphantly, is either not all-kind or not all-powerful; and the theologian must be left to wriggle off the dilemma as best he can. At the same time, it is odd that anyone, appalled by the suffering of sentient things, should rush to an extreme, as Thomas Hardy did, and assume that if any conscious being is responsible for arranging the conditions of life as we know them, that being must be more like a devil than a god. They forget that this Something must also be given credit for all that is pleasant in existence, for the response to beauty (whatever beauty may be) which resides in man, for his love-nature and for the far-stretching might of his intellect. And who shall say whether pleasure or pain preponderates in sentient existence? Gautama was much more aware of its pain than of its pleasure: but I have always found that the difficulty in getting Western people to weigh Buddhism seriously lies in the fact that they cannot accept its initial axiom that all existence is painful. To exist may be painful, they reply, but it is also pleasant.

Perhaps it was this acute sense of suffering which caused the Buddha to hint that there is no God, and that the visible world is both an illusion and radically evil: but " absorption into Nirvana " is ultimately the same conception as the longing of the Persian and Christian mystics to be re-united with the whole of things or, in other words, to be lost in God. Most people, I think, will feel that the Buddha was wise when he told his disciples not to waste their thought upon a fruitless inquiry concerning the origin of all things. Nevertheless, we are insatiably curious, and that question will recur as long as there is a man to form it.

Putting aside all modern refinements, we can say that somehow or other we find ourselves contemplating an universe in which there is time, space, matter, force and consciousness. (The words that we use to describe the contents of the universe are of no importance in this context.) And whenever we ponder the question, we shall find ourselves ending up with a conviction that Something must have " pulled the trigger." We are not in a position to guess whether It cares what happens to Its universe or whether It has any aim in mind: but if I were a materialist, I should be perpetually bothered by the evidence of pattern in the universe, by the apparent purposefulness of the evolutionary process and, most of all, by the difficulty of accounting for the existence of anything whatsoever.

" THE mist of familiarity," wrote Shelley, " obscures from us the wonder of our being." And indeed most people never realise that there is any " wonder " in the fact that they exist. On the contrary, they very soon become used to being alive and to looking out at the world and the stars. Life stupefies them as though it were a heavy narcotic; and it is because they are never even half-awake that they glance at the sun merely in order to see if the weather will be good, and that they find nothing queer in the existence of men or stars or trees. That, they would say, is just how " things " are. Of course there is a sun, and of course there are trees and men.

I want, however, to suggest in these next pages that such men and women are instances of arrested development—in fact, that they are literally stillborn souls. For many people would say of themselves, with Robert Louis Stevenson, that they will " never become really accustomed to being here." Many people have known, for example, the strange experi-

ence of ceasing—perhaps for one instant only—
to take " things " for granted. In that instant
the moon, it may be, will startle them as much
as if it had never before appeared; and then,
when the instant has gone, it will become
once more just an object that is as familiar as
the clock on the mantelpiece. And, for the
matter of that, I had, long ago, a well-loved
friend who worked, and worked effectively, on
the Stock Exchange. He told me that now and
again while he was shouting prices among the
other shouting brokers, he would wake up for
one instant, experience that same feeling, and
see himself and the men about him as agitated
phantoms in a fantastic dream. The life-
embedded man will term this experience
" morbid." The semi-scientific man might
call it " pathological." I am confident that it
is neither: that, on the contrary, those who
have not known it are like kittens before their
eyes are unsealed.

When Plato said that " wonder is the beginning of wisdom," he may have meant merely
that if it were not for curiosity we should have
acquired no scientific knowledge. That, I
know, is how the university-minded would
interpret his words, but I suspect that he meant
much more. The phrase has a notable likeness to one of the " Traditional Sayings of
Jesus," a declaration mysterious and deep:

" He that wonders shall reign, and he that reigns shall rest. Look with wonder on that which is before you." It is possible that until a man ceases to take " things " for granted, as we take for granted the irrational contents of a dream, he is still an embryo-soul, and that this waking-up from life, at which I have tried to hint, is literally the beginning of birth as a spiritual being.

Everyone knows, because bygone scientists demonstrated the fact, that a human embryo briefly recapitulates the history of its human and pre-human ancestors: that the embryo, at a certain stage, has vestigial gills and, at another stage, an unmistakable tail. At seven months (if I remember rightly) the embryo has passed through all its pre-human history and can be born as a human body: nor until then, presumably, could it manifest a human mind. All this we know because men became scientific and wanted to see " how the wheels go round "; and if we muse with emotion and imagination upon this fragment of knowledge, we shall quickly realise its " wonder." You that are reading and I that am writing have bodies around us which in a few months have lived through the changes of many thousands of years: but no one seems to have asked himself why the body should repeat the history of all life, though the why of things is much more significant than the how. It is also a question which is much more difficult to answer. Science, concentrating upon the mechanism of things, can announce definite and reasonably certain results. When we go further and ask ourselves, about anything, why it should be so, we are usually beyond the range of science. If we are right in divining that a man is a body, a life and a soul or spirit, and that the long process which we call the evolution of species is really a gradual involution of spirit within life and body, then we might conclude that the body in its embryonic period is working itself up to the stage at which it will be able to admit the new element of spirit, and that it needs to elaborate itself from its very simplest form for the same reason that a group of actors must always begin with a vague reading of a play before their rendering of it becomes, after many rehearsals, a rich and subtle performance.

For many years I have had a suspicion—apparently entertained with enthusiasm by that lone and brilliant forerunner of the future, James Hinton—that when a child's body has been duly born, the mind within it proceeds to recapitulate the mental history of humanity, nor should I be surprised if psychologists of the bolder kind should some day lend powerful support to this idea. Whether babies really clutch at the moon, I cannot say. If they do, then it must be because all outside things are to them a flat picture; because their minds have not taught their eyes to acquire a sense of perspective or distance; because, in consequence, the bright little object in the sky seems to them as close as any bright little object that is only a few inches away from their noses. At least we know that for some years children cannot clearly or continuously distinguish between something which is in their minds and something which is outside their bodies. Just as the baby's eyes do not focus correctly, so is it in turn with the mind which is a baby. It cannot correctly focus what philosophers call the objective as opposed to the subjective.

And then, a little later, the child will sometimes not believe that external objects may refuse to act as he desires them to act. I know, for example, a woman of uncommon intelligence who once, as a little girl, was blowing bubbles through a clay pipe. Her nurse warned her to be careful not to drop the pipe because it would break and then there would be no more bubbles. The little girl frowned with annoyance and retorted that, if she willed it not to do so, the pipe would certainly not break, and when she put her belief to the test she was astonished by the independent behaviour of her pipe. In the same spirit a witch-doctor will command the clouds to give up their rain; and if we read in *The Golden Bough* of what Frazer called " sympathetic magic," we shall recognise (most of us) queer likenesses to some of our own childish experiences. In one tribe, I remember, a woman was told to walk naked round a corn-sown field, the primitive agriculturist saying to himself that a woman, being a fertile creature, will convey her fertility to the field. Many people can recall the quaint tabus which, as children, they placed upon themselves, or the improvised ceremonies which they performed in order to exorcise fear : as, for instance, that they must run up a certain number of stairs before a door closes behind them if they would escape some vague but horrible catastrophe, or must whisper a meaningless incantation if they would not be molested by the bogies in the bedroom cupboard.

Again, we can recognise the warrior-phase of human history in the period when a normal male-child's chief passion is for mimic battles and for slaughtering battalions of toy-soldiers, an employ in which he engages with an Assyrian or Babylonian ferocity. Then, later, with the coming of early school-days we see the child passing quickly through a stage that corresponds with the time when the advance-guard of humanity was devising alphabets, beginning to study more of arithmetic than ten fingers can teach, and learning curiously about its past. Later still, there is a marked resemblance between the sudden expansion of intelligence, the delight in the body and the awakening to beauty and art which most people experience at puberty and the same characteristics as they showed themselves, on a national scale, in the civilisation of classical Greece. Moreover, those adolescent excitements usually die down within a few years; most people smile at the recollection that they once wrote verse, and once, for a little while, supposed that they were "interested in art." They immerse themselves in what they now call "real life." It is just as though the mind of European man passed through its brief, exciting and troublous adolescence in Athens; as though it then came of age, and applied itself to the typical tasks of early manhood, in the law-making, world-mastering genius of the Romans; as though Athens had been our public school or university and Rome the business-world in which we had subsequently settled down. The very homosexuality of the classical Greeks may have been a symptom that the European mind was adolescent. The Athenian man's admiration for the beauty of other men may correspond with the narcissan delight which many boys experience when they emerge from childhood.

Here we see the mind of Europe developing from animism and magic to polytheism; from the childish polytheism of Homer to the fine-spun idealism of Plato; and from this in turn to the materialism of the Roman stoics; and the European cycle has a general likeness to the mental stages which a normal man traverses between infancy and the age, let us say, of thirty. At the end of this cycle Rome disintegrated and collapsed. Orthodox historians have suggested various causes, economic and political, for the Decline and Fall, and obviously that Decline and Fall must have been accompanied by certain unfavourable circumstances; but if we imagine for a few moments that human affairs are not influenced only by external conditions, but are ultimately the effects of spiritual forces which work from behind the visible world, we may perceive that the Roman Empire, like a man whose mind has reached its boundaries when he is thirty, disintegrated because the European soul had progressed as far as it could in its Greco-Roman form or body. And we shall not be surprised if those men of Europe, those parts of the European soul, that had still to emerge from infancy proceeded to catch up with the others and actually, like an acorn dropped by an oak, to develop through noticeably similar stages. There was, of course, one difference.

Christianity had come into Europe: Christianity with its call to the sympathy and love which were latent in man, and with its conception of One God. This conception had arisen, long ago, in Vedic India, as we can see if we look at the *Hymn to the One that has no Name*; and in Egypt, as early as the Fourth Dynasty, aristocratic persons, at least, appear to have grasped it. What other meaning can we perversely read into this magnificent passage from a *Hymn to Ra*? " O Divine Youth, who art self-created, I cannot comprehend thee. Thou art the Lord of heaven and earth, and didst create beings celestial and beings terrestrial. Thou art the god One, who camest into being in the beginning of time. . . Thou art unknowable, and no tongue can describe thy similitude; thou existest alone. Millions of years have passed over the world. I cannot tell the number of those through which thou hast passed. Thou journeyest through spaces, requiring millions of years to pass over, in one little moment of time; and then thou settest and dost make an end of the hours." After the breakdown of Roman civilisation, then, an event of major importance had happened within the growing soul of Europe. There had been, in fact, a definite " change of heart," and for that reason the new cycle was not a mere repetition of the old, as if humanity were a bluebottle that ceaselessly climbs up the window, drops and then climbs again.

Still, we can hardly miss the resemblance. First there are those men of the Dark Ages— the Merovingians, the Carlovingians and innumerable others—who behaved like greedy, quarrelsome children in whom conscience was only a bud. Then, in the Middle Ages, the mind of Europe, with the Pope for Headmaster, again goes to school and elaborates an intricate theological system. Next, in the Italian Renascence, as earlier in ancient Greece, the men of the new cycle achieve their own adolescence, and another fountain of vitality rushes up through the mind, and they put away their theological toys: until at length, looking upon ourselves, we recognise the same tendency towards materialism in thought and externalisation of interest which, because they experienced it before us, makes the Romans more akin to us than any people that has lived in the world.

The science of the future may demonstrate, much better than I can, that the mind is an embryo for years after the body has finished and forgotten its embryonic recapitulation; and it is because I am presumptuously trying to take science by the forelock—because

I believe that some day men will perceive all this to be true—it is for that reason that I wrote just now of stillborn souls: for if it is true, and if the things of the physical world imitate the things of the spiritual world, then it is clear that a great many people stop short when they have mentally developed up to the general level of their race and time. Of them we can say, with Rossetti:

" They die not—for their life was death—but cease,"

for, having completed their recapitulation of the mind's history, they cannot achieve birth as independent souls. Their bodies continue to live for many years, but spiritually they make no advance because they are dead.

Such people are drugged, as I have said, by life, and accept the existence of the world and their own existence without wonder, without meditation, so that they live their sixty or seventy years as mere repetitive bits in the machinery of life and the world. They remain imprisoned within the limits of mind and soul which bound their period. They dare not think or believe or imagine or divine beyond the intellectual convention of their age, precisely as they dare not dress or behave beyond its social conventions. Every one of us, no doubt, is circumscribed by the age into which he is born, but it is a tame spirit that will make no effort to grow beyond it and to see things as they may be seen in the future.

It is strange indeed that the very persons— the young men and women—who most violently rebel against the conventional morality or the social order of our time rarely rebel against its intellectual conventions. A young man will decide to think out for himself the question of companionate marriages, and will proceed to scrape off, so far as he can, the barnacles of bygone thought which are still clinging to his mind. He does his utmost to look at the subject with new and unprejudiced eyes. He will also lecture in the communist cause. But if he considers the problem of the universe and of his own existence, he usually accepts without challenge the mechanistic bias of scientific doctrine. If he would be a revolutionary not only in respect of morality but also of philosophy, and would try to see everything with new and unprejudiced eyes, he would in all likelihood make certain surprising discoveries, and might end by suspecting that science is only an auxiliary to religion and a check upon fantasy.

We get the knowledge which we call science by observation and subsequent deduction. It can be taught and learned. We get religious knowledge only by experience, for religion is a state of mind, emotionally-tinged, that comes out of our observation and deduction as a flower comes out of the leaves that enfold it. Most of the inward turmoil from which men have suffered was due to the simple fact that we are both feeling and thinking creatures. We confuse the two functions, and that is why the man of religion vainly tries to make his feelings into a science which he calls theology, and why the man of science vainly tries to make an entire philosophy out of observation and deduction. A religious use of the mind could never have informed us that the moon is two hundred and seventy thousand miles from the earth: but for a very long time our ancestors, having much religious feeling and hardly any observed knowledge, put forward their dreams and guesses as if they were statements of fact. Consider only for how many centuries men and women accepted the story of Adam and Eve, or the story of Jonah, as if it were scientific knowledge. The man of science, on the contrary, observes and thinks, but at that point he stops. If he would then allow his feelings to take their natural course, he might find himself on the brink of religion. There would be, in truth, no foolish tug-of-war between religion and science if men could realise, in this way, that religion ought to be a meditation upon science, that science is actually the material upon which religion must be founded, and that (to put it another way) the more sound knowledge we obtain, the more significant will be our emotions about it. Much religious feeling has been based upon faulty observation. Shallow people, proud of their corrected observation, instantly decide, when they realise this truth, that religious feeling must be worthless: but the richer our knowledge, the richer our feeling about it ought to be. A primitive man, for example, was often awe-struck by the menstruation of women, and proceeded to think about it quite wrongly. A modern doctor, or we might even say a modern man, thinks about it correctly, and for that very reason supposes that there is no mystery attached to it. Once again he has been satisfied to discover the How and does not proceed to ponder the Why.

We should think ourselves much more astonishing and mysterious creatures if we were not satisfied merely to collect facts. A man's body, for example, begins when a male-cell, or spermatozoon, coalesces with a female cell, or ovum. Consider, though, what that spermatozoon is: how it is one of an immense number which the father of the new child is carrying in his body: how every man in the world is carrying thousands of these drops of life: how incalculable is their ancestry, for the life in every man must necessarily be descended from the first life that ever pulsed in the world; and how each of those life-drops has within it the possibility of growing into a man with (as we say) the "same" nose, the same knee-cap, the same ear-form and perhaps many of the same likes and dislikes, the same moods and thoughts, as those of the man in whose body it resided. Indeed, as a first experiment in mystical feeling I would recommend a man to look at the hand of his son, especially if it is like his own, and to reflect that the whole body of that younger man (together with who knows how much of his emotional being) was once latent partly within his own body and partly within the body of a woman whom for twenty or thirty years of his life he did not know and who, as likely as not, was living a great many miles away from him. And if he proceeds to reflect upon the incontrovertible fact that his son's hand, like his own, is the last of many millions of forms which existed before it, having a pedigree that goes back to the beginning of all life, then he must be entirely devoid of imagination, of the power to see beyond the immediate, if he does not realise that to be alive is exceedingly strange.

From this meditation he can easily progress to another: for what is true of human spermatozoa and their immense ancestry is true also of every living creature or plant. Everything at which we look to-day—this very day, and no matter whether we are in the town or the country—is a last link in a chain of lives which, humanly speaking, is endless. But so far as we can judge, it is only human beings, and unfortunately not all of them, that have also this peculiar power of getting mentally outside the vast and ancient life-stream in which, like everything else, they find themselves: they only who can be at once in it physically and a looker-on at it mentally. Any man who will ask himself how it is that he, a life-creature, has developed this faculty of standing aside from life, as a half-awakened dreamer will sometimes half-realise that he is in bondage to a dream, may experience a feeling that there is a part of him which is not under the dominion of life and in consequence not under sentence of death. And this indeed may have been the thought at which a forgotten poet was grasping when he wrote

that "Nothing which can see death, dies"—
that, in fact, it is because there is something
deathless within us that we are aware, as
other creatures apparently are not, that death
will put out our lives.

XII

A SENSIBLE man will hold a few ideas firmly, believing in them partly on account of the evidence and partly because they " ring true " upon his whole mind, of which intellect is only an aspect; but he will also hold other ideas provisionally, judging them to be possibly or even probably true. We might, for example, feel sure that personality survives death, although all but the spiritual core of it will fall away in a succession of after-deaths in other " worlds," and yet, though confident of this, be not more than seriously inclined to accept the ancient doctrine of reincarnation.

We have to clear away rubbish of various kinds before we can even examine the subject fairly. There is the emotional rubbish of the many people who " believe in reincarnation " because it amuses their vanity or their fancy : a group which includes all the shallow-minded folk who relish the flattering daydream that they were once Cleopatra. The soul of Cleopatra would need to have been broken up into several thousands of pieces if all claimants to it were to be satisfied. Again, there is another kind of emotional rubbish—a kind well illustrated by a clergyman (of considerable position, in his day), who said to me once, " I could never believe in reincarnation. Life is too painful. I don't wish to live again " : an attitude which is just as absurd as a denial of gravitation because we do not like falling upon hard surfaces. It is imperative to get rid of the notion that reincarnation is a mystical doctrine, occult, weird, uncanny or sentimental. Reincarnation, if it happens to be true, is merely a natural law, a piece of mechanism by which life acts. Again, there is the theological objection, based upon the fact that Christianity (at least since the time of Origen) has never endorsed the belief. We can see how shallow this objection is if we reflect that Christianity never announced that the solar system is heliocentric, nor shall we find in its exposition any reference to gravitation or to the nature of an atom. And yet again there is the objection that " nobody can really remember a past life."

Let us take this objection separately, because it is the commonest. In the first place, we cannot state so definitely that no one has ever remembered a past life. Pythagoras was said to have recognised a set of arms and armour as having been his in a previous existence. There are several stories, apparently well authenticated, of Eastern children who have recognised their former parents. There is, in Maeterlinck's notable essay *Our Eternity*, a striking account of some prolonged experiments in hypnotism conducted by a reputable Frenchman. His patient, a young woman, was led back in trance to her earliest childhood and then to infancy, then into a pre-natal darkness, then to the end of a previous life in which she assumed the character of an old man who described his native town and the course of his life, and then again to a yet earlier life in which the patient was once more a woman. We may dismiss the whole story by saying that the woman was an ingenious fraud or by saying that her apparently different selves were only examples of dissociated personality; and although we might possibly be right, we have no justification whatever for preferring an alternative explanation to the one that is most obvious. Moreover, Buddhism declares that any man, if he strenuously and continuously exercises his memory, can ultimately drive it across the darkness of infancy, birth and pre-natal existence, and recover the sensations of his last death. Indeed, this development of memory is one of the simpler and most ordinary practices in mind-training which are used in Buddhist monasteries of the better kind.[1]

Most of these objections are based upon a careless misunderstanding of the idea. Our memories of a past life could very seldom be of evidential value. Of what significance were it for me to state that about 3500 B.C. I was a son of a high Egyptian official, that I killed a lion when I was fifteen, that subsequently I led a military expedition, that I married a comely girl, studied astrology and died at the age of sixty-seven? None at all, for nobody could verify my statements: but consider—most lives are even less memorable than this one. There is, in fact, very little experience in any man's life which is not connected with trivial or at least with entirely temporary interests: very little, we might even say, which is not connected with his bodily pains and pleasures. How much do we remember of our deeds and emotions five, ten, twenty years ago? If I ask you, "What were you doing and feeling in the autumn of 1923?" your answer will be exceedingly vague. And yet even if death be but "a moment's storm or not so much," it is a catastrophic event. It severs the mind from the brain: the brain in which for so many years the mind has been

[1] See *The Wisdom of the Aryas*, by Allan Bennett, pp. 101–104.

accustomed to work as well as it can. During our present life we have undergone no such violent or fundamental disorganisation, and yet we can offer only the sketchiest outlines of our recent experience.

For my part I should be so cautious as not even to deny that a man may remember the form and colour of the tunic which he wore in ancient Rome; but we ought not to demand these minute and precise recollections. If I sit down to play a game of chess, I find awaiting me a certain aptitude for the game. I do not remember the many hundreds of chess-games which I played as a lad. It is from them, however, that I derive some measure of skill. Similarly, between death and a new birth, our specific memories of the life which that death ended may well resolve themselves into general aptitudes, nor should we expect any effects more definite.

Most people in this age of intellect, this age that requires every intuition to be proved as we can prove a theory about some physical phenomenon, will be happier in the belief that a man's personality may be attributed to his heredity and environment. They are certainly upon very safe ground; for seeing that every man's heredity goes back to the beginning of life in this world, it is easy to account vaguely for any characteristic by assuming that it is a throw-back to a remote ancestor—one or other of the millions who are behind each of us. To say this, however, is not to prove it: and if we have no temperamental prejudice against the theory that reincarnation is a natural law, we shall probably find more difficulty in accounting for the Greek instinct of John Keats by referring it to his heredity and environment than by supposing that he made use of aptitudes and a temperament which had their roots in ancient Greece itself.

It is not at all impossible that scientists will some day confirm the principle of reincarnation, though they could do so only after a long and severe struggle with the infatuated sceptic. If someone, remembering a past life, should enable archæologists to recover the lost books of Livy or to find a statue by Praxiteles that was drowned in a shipwreck, we should witness a lively combat between the professors of various theories; but there can be little doubt of the verdict at which the ordinary reasonable, unprejudiced man would arrive. Reincarnation, in a word, may be as true as any accepted natural law: it may be working automatically at the present moment and have been so working ever since life and form were associated: but even if this were a fact, it might easily slip through the mesh of intellect, because it usually covers too wide a span of time for any normal person to be able to detect it.

The typical modern man is not able to take the matter seriously for the simple reason that he does not believe that any part of a personality will survive death. If, on the contrary, we do believe that some part of us will survive, we have once more to get rid of the old supposition that death leaves the entire personality unimpaired. This, we have seen, is in the highest degree improbable, if only because the greater part of the mind is developed by its earthly conditions and could only be of any use in this particular world. We should therefore be childish if we supposed that Leonardo da Vinci could reappear at the present time as, in all details, precisely the same personality: but someone might have birth in A.D. 2000 in whom the general aptitudes and tendencies of Leonardo should be manifested again.

Assuming (since we cannot for ever be starting from the same point) that there is a principle in man which " hath elsewhere its dwelling and cometh from afar "—that there is something to which death is irrelevant— then it is at least possible that forces from that spiritual dimension or universe or state-of-being are for ever entering the visible world and for ever returning home again, and that they are connected with physical forms by the ebbing and flowing of that mysterious medium which we call life.

XIII

IT is not so difficult, we sometimes feel, to think that there may be a spiritual and deathless principle in men if we are personally at ease. The soul may seem to be a possibility to a man who is meditating in a London house or flat: for although there are plenty of cunning scoundrels in London, and plenty of violent ruffians, they are kept so well in hand that we are startled if once in a twelvemonth some ruffian kills an old woman or if a scoundrel of the more ambitious kind is brought by law to the surface. The soul, we feel, might seem remote indeed if we were dwelling in a country where private or political murders are committed by the hundred, or in a more violent age when a man's life was held, at least by many, as cheaply as the life of a fly or blackbeetle. England is among the most civilised of countries, and by this I mean that in England a man in sudden distress may hope with some confidence to find sympathy and help from his fellows. Here, not in material achievement, lies the measure of a community's civilisation.

In thinking about the soul, then, it is necessary to realise that we see it very seldom. All kindly people manifest it to some extent, but it is only seen at all strikingly in the saint who has reduced selfishness to a minimum. Most of us act, nearly always, as vehicles of mere life; nor are we altogether to blame. The industrial society which our forefathers built up, and of which we are often proud, is of a kind which forces most men to fight for themselves and against others. Our social system prevents the spiritual part of us from finding more than a few small opportunities of showing itself. We are too busy with our buying and selling, our necessary effort to extract a livelihood from a hostile or at least unhelpful society. We have, as we say, " no time " to think about the soul; and it seems to us, therefore, that to speculate about the soul is a luxury which only the well-to-do can afford.

Again, we must admit that it is not easy in our particular age to champion the conception of a soul in man. The current is against us. Think only of those writers who, in England alone, are now most popular, most nearly intellectual leaders, among serious people. Shaw, Wells, Aldous Huxley, Bertrand Russell—names which may look exceedingly small in the twenty-first century—these are the men who, acting as distributors for the science of their day, are perhaps (in England) the most influential whom we could cite. In their works they give no suggestion of believing that there is a spiritual element in men which will outlast death. Not one of them, I believe, would deny that he regards a man as no more than a combination of chemicals. And in consequence both they and their innumerable followers expect a future that shall be even more thoroughly dominated by a materialistically-scientific view than the present is. Perhaps they are right. If so, then I am an antediluvian dreamer, a fit companion for the late Bishop Wilberforce, and might just as well write a book with the purpose of proving that the earth is flat as a book which attempts to suggest that the soul, after all, is a reality. But an alternative remains—that, improbable as it seems at the moment, they are all slaves of their time, and that when they are dead they will have a surprise much greater than the greatest surprise of their lives.

We look at modern Russia, and there we see a society—a huge society—which, if we except the brief mood of the French Revolution, is the first to abandon explicitly the ancient conceptions of a God and of a soul. A great part of our intelligentsia regards Russia as the courageous forerunner of the future man : the sensible, materialistic, science-worshipping, spirit-denying man. Again, they may be right : but they may also be counting their chickens before the eggs have been hatched. We are often told that the violence of a political revolution is in proportion to the severity of the system which it overthrows; and modern Russia is a striking example of this likely principle. Our complacent materialists, however, are strangely blind to a factor in the Russian situation which to some of us appears unmistakable. We know that the Russian people before the revolution were, however superstitiously, perhaps the most religious people in Europe. Religious feeling, whether we think it comes from a profound source or is merely the effect of an immensely long inheritance, cannot easily be extirpated from the minds of men; and when we watch a government suppressing that instinct with a severity at least as extreme as the severity with which the Tsarist government suppressed the desire for liberty, we must be simple-minded, however " brilliant " in other matters, if we do not foresee that this ancient instinct will some day produce a new revolution, and that the religious revolution will be as violent as the suffocation of religion which it will overthrow. Fifty thousand Russians will fall to the machine-guns of an atheistic government. Fifty thousand more will starve to death for their belief. But the cause of the martyr seldom fails, and the nineteenth-century Russians (or Father Gapon himself) who died for liberty would be the most fervent supporters of this proposition. If the fashionable thinkers of our time are right, we (or our children) will all become communists, and science will have buried religion for ever: for the Russians have merely put into practice the unreligious view of life which Europeans, although that view is general among them, have not been sufficiently thoroughgoing to express. If they are wrong, then we shall see in Russia a revival of Christianity on a scale and of an intensity which have never been witnessed since Christianity was a young religion.

These may at present seem "wild and whirling words." They may seem a little less whirling if we turn to an article [1] which I happened to read within an hour of writing them. "The distinguished Russian exile, Professor Nicholas Berdyaev," I read, "who as an ex-Marxist has written with great insight on the psychology of Russian Communism,

[1] Mr. A. J. Penty in *The New English Weekly*.

asserts that it can be comprehended only as a religion striving to take the place of Christianity." " It is," says the Professor,[1] " the religion of the kingdom of this world, the last and final denial of the other world, of every kind of spirituality. That is precisely the reason why its very materialism becomes spiritual and mystical. The Communist State is quite different from the ordinary secular State. It is a theocratic State which takes over the functions that belong to the Church. It forms men's souls, gives them an obligatory creed, demands their whole soul, exacts from them not only ' what is Cæsar's ' but even ' what is God's.' It is most important to grasp this pseudo-theocratic nature of the Communist State. Its whole structure is determined by it. It is a system of extreme monism, in which there is no distinction between State, Society and Church."

In trying to foresee what will happen in Russia, we must remember that science is new to the average Russian mind, and that the first impact of the scientific revelation is always exciting and subversive. At the present time it is capturing the adolescent intellect not only of Russia but also of the Far East. Were I speaking among those who assume that the future must be merely an intensification of

[1] In *The Russian Revolution*, p. 88.

the present, I should ask them to make an imaginative effort. I should ask them to conceive of the changes that would follow if, at one date or another, the tyrants who maintain the materialistic direction of Russian life, were themselves to be seriously disquieted by a suspicion that materialism is a fallacy. I should ask them to imagine the possibility that science itself may achieve the difficult task of establishing the existence of the soul, and the further possibility that to do so may be the destiny of the Russian intellect. And then I should ask them whether the revolution which would follow that discovery would not be, of necessity, the most influential that the world has ever witnessed and one that would make all political revolutions appear trivial.

XIV

MEANWHILE, assuming, as I must, that the soul is a reality, and that in consequence it cannot be denied for ever, I see that any religion of the future will be simple in its outlines. It is the busy-body intellect which complicates religion; and now that intellect is wide-awake the world will never again adhere to a complex theology. We shall admit at last that religion and science pertain to different parts of the mind. We shall not return to an anthropomorphic conception of God, but we shall probably agree that time, space and the universe could not be here around us, and could not continue, unless there were at the core of all existence Something which we may just as well call God: a Something which was the origin of the laws that sustain the universe; which is no more like the mind of a man than like the energy of a meteor: Something, therefore, to which we can appeal only in so far as it is itself partly human and the basis of human consciousness. We shall recognise that the life in the body is no more the soul of a man than the body is; that the soul is a late-comer into the world; and that it is engaged in an uphill struggle with the forces of matter and the instinct of life. We shall see that it flickers intermittently through the apparatus which we call our bodies and their life-force. We shall see it as a ray of light that goes wavering downward through the dense medium of water, a thing or a force or an influence which, like the ray of light as perceived by a fish, comes from a different and unimaginable element. We shall discern its presence wherever we find sympathy, love and a sense of union with the same principle in other objects; and we shall neither be overwhelmed by the immensity of an universe which has no power over the soul because the soul does not belong to it, nor surprised or unduly dejected by the grim record of humanity, knowing that the devilries of men are the handiwork of the life-instinct and not of the slowly-entering soul. When we think of the men and women who went down on the *Titanic* and, according to all reports, awaited death with composure and perhaps with exaltation, we shall realise that not all men act basely, and that these men at least, in the ordeal of those hours, may well have become conscious that they were more than living organisms.

PART III

I

THE man who writes upon sexual morality is thrusting his hand into a bed of nettles, for the two topics which awaken most passion and prejudice among our contemporaries are the claims of communism and the claims of women. A really young thinker will suppose that nothing could possibly be more important than the type of social organisation under which we are all destined to live. Indeed, there are people who tell us that we have been absurdly exaggerating the significance of sexual conduct and that we ought to regard it as a factor in life which is interesting but not important. They would have us think of it, in fact, as no more than a branch of hygiene. They smile at the tremendous ado which people made in the past about adultery, and assure us that the enlightened husband or wife should tolerate an infidelity, and even perhaps recognise that it may be as beneficial to the health of a marriage as a holiday by the sea may be beneficial to the health of the body. Such people are well-meaning theorists who fancy that they can ignore the deep, fierce power of primitive emotion and can rationalise their sexuality without ultimate disaster. Some of them doubtless succeed in rationalising the primitive, but only because their emotional natures are tepid. Others find out, too late, that their possessiveness and natural jealousy were stronger than they had fancied, and that a doctrine which is practicable for those of anæmic emotion is useless to the normal man or woman. Such a view of sexuality is based, as a rule, upon some acquaintance with modern science, especially biology, and of course upon an assumption that there is no spiritual principle in man. The strong wish of those that preach it is " to be sensible about sex "; and what, for example, could be more " sensible " than an occasional exchange of wives and husbands? Even thirty years ago a party of four Fabians—two married pairs—went into Italy for a holiday, and only an indignant refusal from one of the wives prevented an amicable reassortment of sleeping-partners for a month or six weeks. This young wife was disappointingly primitive, and it will be part of our enterprise to discover whether she was wise or foolish. At least we can say at once that the thinker may be wrong when he assumes that communism is a more important topic than sexual conduct, for there was wisdom in the observation of Dr. Johnson that no change of government causes a man to eat or sleep less well: while everyone knows, on the contrary, that the sleep and the appetite of many millions have been impaired by the behaviour of a housemate.

Perhaps, though, people will not continue for much longer to live as housemates at all? Our typical intellectuals, ignoring the fate of the French Revolution, conceive that Russian Communism is founded in rock; that what Russia does to-day, the world will do to-morrow; that in consequence neither marriage nor the family will exist for more than another generation or two; and that children, brought up in colossal crêches, will be supported partly by the wage-earning parents and partly by the taxpayer under his august name of " The State." It is true that all this may happen; true that men and women may miraculously settle down to the flatness of an uncompetitive life; and true also that the intellectual type, constitutionally dissatisfied with any existing order, would probably rebel more vigorously than any other against an arrangement which it now advocates. Assuming, however, that our intellectuals are merely charmed by a neat pattern into which unruly humanity will never fit for long, I propose to consider the immediate future of sexual morality as though the present order of occidental society were destined to undergo none but gradual changes.

Again, it is obvious that no one can say anything about sexual behaviour that shall be true of all conditions and ages; and yet if we avoid any generalisations and satisfy the pedant by qualifying every sentence, we become as irritating as a man with a nervous cough. Among savages, for instance, a wife is often a drudge rather than a companion : a fact which led one writer to say that in primitive communities "it is commonly the wife who incites the husband to add to the number of his wives, no doubt with a view to lightening her domestic burdens. In short," he continues, "when marriage means, for a woman, chiefly doing her husband's work, she desires to share her husband with other women; where, as with ourselves, it means chiefly spending her husband's income, her feelings are violated by the thought of it." [1] Even in an English "working-class" family, the wife is often cook, housemaid, wife and mother, a condition which makes marriage very different from what it is in leisured or professional or business society. Among the French, too, the wife,

[1] John Langdon-Davies in his stimulating and informative book *A Short History of Women* (p. 133). The book is, in general, more feministic in tone than this tart quotation will suggest.

bringing her " dot," makes a marriage much more of an economic partnership than it is in England, Germany or the United States. I can only rely upon the reader, therefore, to perceive the extent to which any generalisation is meant to apply: and after these preliminaries, I suggest that we should try to take our bearings amidst the moral confusion of the present age.

II

IF we want to understand how sexual morality has altered during the present century, and how it is likely to develop, we cannot do better than compare the world as it is with the world as it was. With this purpose in view, then, let us again invoke the image of our imaginary Rip van Winkle who fell asleep in 1900 at the age of twenty-five. It is difficult, no doubt, to imagine a London without aeroplanes, tube-railways, motor-buses, films and wireless, but it is even more difficult to recapture a sense of how in those days men thought about women and how women thought about themselves.

The sexes hardly shared life at all. Women were expected to be thoroughly feminine and men to be thoroughly masculine. The sight of a girl at the wheel of a motor-car would have made anyone dubious about her general decency; [1] and the sight of a nun so occupied —I see one driving past my window at this

[1] Arnold Bennett in his *Journal* (1917) mentions that he has seen " girls driving cars."

moment—would have startled the world not less than if the Prince of Wales were to give an acrobatic turn in one of Mr. Cochran's revues. Women were still supposed to be incapable of practical activity except in the management of a house. They were, indeed, expected to be so helpless and so unstained by the world that there was a certain charm in their inability to understand how to draw a cheque. Perhaps there is no more conspicuous change that has occurred within the last thirty years than the freer association of the sexes and the consequent decline of an emphatic type in either. I knew in my boyhood men who were so pronouncedly masculine that they had nothing to say in mixed company; but as years have gone by, men of this extreme type have steadily become fewer until now, when there are scarcely any interests which men and women do not share, society has no place for them. They have become as anachronistic as three-bottle men at the time when nightly drunkenness had gone out of fashion.

A young man in 1900 regarded a young woman as a foreigner; assumed that her thoughts and emotions were as different from his own as the Russian language is from English; and looked upon her as being in all ways less capable than he, as needing protection from other men, but also as giving to life a flavour of the ideal. For him, we must remember, women were either completely good or bad. They were either loose women or ladies; and he had only a formal knowledge of lady-girls. Their interests and his did not overlap. He met them only in a kind of no-man's-land—at dances or at meals; and if at a dance he kissed a lady-girl in the conservatory, both he and she had to think of the kiss as in some degree serious. She was likely to assume that it might be meant as a prelude to marriage; and if he did not marry her, he might have felt more than a little guilty when he met her again. Had her parents heard of it, they would not have allowed him to revisit the house; and if he made a practice of conservatory-kissing, most men would have agreed that he was probably a cad. The average man, in fact, never tried to know a lady-girl well unless he had marriage, however vaguely, in his mind. That segregation of the sexes undoubtedly contributed to the strict sexual morality of the time. The men of the Smart Set, I am told, already looked upon the seduction of other men's wives as a distinguished, because perilous, amusement; and perilous it certainly was, for nobody could socially survive a divorce. To most men, however, there were two clear classes of women: the lady-girls who formed a wife-caste and the others—whom no self-respecting man would ever have thought of marrying.

All lady-girls were presumed to be chaste. They had either to marry or to settle down to life-long celibacy. The alternatives were so definite that nobody thought of life-long celibacy as being, for a woman, unnatural or difficult or dangerous. And women, by reason of a feminine characteristic which we shall be considering a few minutes later, submitted to it as unprotestingly as Chinese women of that time to the distortion of their feet. Purity was, indeed, essential in a lady-girl. If she had lost her virginity—a rare state—she was very unlikely to marry; and if she did marry, having probably suppressed the truth, she would have had the devil to pay for the rest of her life. The man who jeopardised her marriage chance had, therefore, quite literally "ruined" her, and everyone, without exception, would have agreed that he was unquestionably a cad.

With chastity so highly valued, extreme physical modesty was universal in the wife-caste. They had no legs and no breasts—only skirts and indeterminate "bosoms." Dr. Wingfield Stratford [1] cites an account of some young ladies in a boat who permitted a man-swimmer to drown because they were too shy

[1] *The Victorian Sunset.*

to bring him naked out of the water—an incident, I gather, of the eighteen-'eighties: and in the very year which we have in mind, the year 1900, a lady, returning with us from an hour on the sea in a row-boat, caused much difficulty but no surprise by modestly refusing either to paddle ashore or to consign herself to the arms of the boatman.

Rip van Winkle, waking up in 1930 or a few years earlier, would not have believed his eyes or his ears. What would he have seen? Holiday-girls bathing and sunning themselves in scanty and skin-tight costumes, river-girls in the shortest of " shorts," chorus-girls with bare legs, bare waists and bare backs. Wherever he went, indeed, he would find this girl and that girl, in millions, acknowledging the existence of their legs and the fact that their " bosoms " have definite form. We cannot conceive his amazement and confusion. Even our posters, even the advertisements in our illustrated weekly papers, would horrify, delight and inflame him.

And what would he have heard? Hair-raising reports of the sexual freedom enjoyed by young people in Scandinavia and in parts of the United States. A sound authority, too, might have told him, instead of me, that the young people in many of our factories regularly pair off for the week-ends without affecting the girl's marriage chance. He would find, too, that a kiss is given and taken with little more seriousness than a handshake. He would be dumbfounded by the knowledge of sexual facts which is possessed by many whom he would judge to be lady-girls, and he would not know how to classify the many young women who regard a sex affair with no solemnity whatever. He might also have met a young novelist of my acquaintance who would have disgusted him by observing, " I should not require my wife to be a virgin. It is much less speculative to marry a girl who has had some experience of men, and I should only take into consideration the personalities of the men to whom she had been a lover." In 1900 men were exceedingly possessive, and proud to be so.

Rip van Winkle, in short, would very soon conclude that in sexual behaviour the typical girls of our period claim an equality with men. He would be even more amazed to learn that many married women maintain the right " to do as they wish with their bodies "; and he would only recover his equilibrium when he realised that most of these wives are more extreme in theory than in practice. Moreover, although the girl who complained of

Ernest's enthusiasm for her body may have been somewhat cruder than the normal girl of our day, Rip van Winkle would quickly realise that the difference between them is not considerable.

ALTHOUGH few of them realised it, the women of Rip van Winkle's youth were conforming to a moral system of almost venerable age; nor should this be at all surprising. A moral system is more stable than anything else in human affairs, and it is easy to understand why it is so, and why morality has so seldom undergone a dramatic change. A man in his youth will decide, perhaps, to walk to his office and to make the homeward journey by omnibus. In middle-age he would be uncomfortable if he did not conform with a practice which by then has become a habit. Morality, as most people use the word, is the habit not of a man but of a community, not of a lifetime but of generations. Unless it is violently interrupted, as a man's personal habit may be interrupted by an illness or a change of environment, this habit of generations will continue for an indefinite time (as in Egypt and China), nor is it any more easily broken than a personal habit. Indeed, it very soon becomes indistinguishable from mere custom, and a primitive community could seldom give any other reason for doing this or for not doing that than the plea that its ancestors behaved in like manner.

The morality of a people, moreover, is obviously due in part to external conditions. We are told, for example, until we are tired of hearing it, that " morality is geographical " —a phrase by which the speaker means, as a rule, that hot climates excite sexual impulse and make nudity or semi-nudity convenient. Morality is also affected, no doubt, by the proportion of males to females and, again, by the sort of life which they are leading. In a nomad community, women, though indispensable, are a handicap, and their status will therefore be low. In a military state, like Sparta or the Prussia of Bismarck, they have to regard themselves as little else than breeders of men. On the other hand, in a new colony they attain almost to goddess-hood because they are few, and their status will therefore be high.

We should probably be right, however, if we decided that the more civilised a people becomes the less will its morality be moulded by conditions. As we develop, morality becomes more mental; and even in a savage community it is formed to a great extent upon ideas. Any book about anthropology shows how often a moral code has been based upon errors of thought. For we should remember that for a long time religion and science are one and the same. They separate only when new and more accurate knowledge conflicts with inherited ideas. We find, for example, that most savages are alarmed by menstrual blood, and that before hunting, fishing or fighting expeditions they will refrain from sexual intercourse for reasons which we regard as superstitious, and that out of their mistaken ideas they have developed elaborate systems of behaviour.

New and more accurate knowledge has been conflicting with our own inherited ideas, and that is the cause of our present confusion. We do not always remember that much of our own morality (using the word, for convenience, in its Anglo-American sense of sexual conduct) descends from the ideas of two persons of such antiquity as Moses and Saint Paul. No one will deny that Moses lived in a society which had not outgrown a superstitious horror of menstruation, or that Saint Paul's ideas were limited by the religious outlook and the scientific knowledge of his time. It is, indeed, an astonishing incident in human history that the ideas of these two men, because they are set forth in the Bible, should have dominated millions and millions of lives for close upon two thousand years, and that only a generation ago the Western world should have been morally oriented by those ideas. If we look back merely across three centuries, we find that Milton's doctrine of the ideal relationship between husband and wife was built upon his belief in the literal truth of the Jewish tale about Adam and Eve.

Now, the moral rules of the mid-Victorian were as solid as his mahogany furniture. He knew (irrespective of what he did) that adultery and fornication were always wrong. Divorce, too, was not only a social disgrace: it was also an offence against God; and the Victorian view might have persisted for centuries if science had not shattered traditional religion and deprived the old rules of their sanction. Science, in this way, must have done much to hasten the emancipation of women, for so long as the world believed the story of Adam and Eve, with its implication that Eve was an inferior creature, and so long as it believed that Saint Paul was divinely inspired, women could not have broken through the colossal wall of public opinion: nor would they have desired to do so. They may have begun, in the days of the French Revolution, by claiming political equality with men, but any judicious observer would have foreseen that in due time they were sure to claim also an economic and a sexual equality. The truth, as we have just seen, is that within the last twenty-five years life, for women, has changed out of recognition. They go into business, they break speed records, they win the King's Prize for rifle-shooting, and are, by comparison with their grandmothers, almost like a third sex. The world, too, has so greatly modified its view of sexual morality that modern women can hardly believe that the Victorian view still dominated society in 1900. Women, while the old morality was dissolving with unprecedented rapidity, not only seized their opportunity of claiming more sexual freedom, but also, as I hope to show, have caught men napping and have landed us all in a grotesque situation. So greatly has the old morality disintegrated that, if habits were not so difficult to break, we should now have no moral rules whatever. Many people of this and the last generation strenuously rebelled against Moses and Saint Paul, but exceedingly few, if any, have been able to free themselves entirely from the old prejudices. There is in human nature a profound inertia which prevents the adoption of any reform until it is overdue by fifty or a hundred years; an infuriating inertia which causes the youthful rebel of each generation to despair of his elders; a blessed inertia which, nevertheless, safeguards humanity from experimenting with the nostrums of the fanatic.

IV

MOST Victorians and very many Edwardians regretfully sigh for the long-drawn
Golden Age of the male which persisted even
into the first decade of our century. The
collapse of the patriarchal system has been so
sudden that it has taken the world unawares;
and all the changes which have followed upon
that collapse have happened to deal out more
power to women and less to men. Gradual
changes had already improved the position of
women, but it is by a mere accident that the
greatest of all their disabilities has recently
vanished in a twinkling.

The age-long subjection of women had
doubtless a great many causes. We can discern without difficulty three advantages which
men had by nature and have lost, wholly or in
part, by civilisation. The first is the fact that
the male is muscularly more powerful than the
female; the second, that men have been better
placed economically because they have been
the money-earners; and the third, that sexual
intercourse has hitherto involved a woman in
possible pregnancy.

The strong man in a primitive society had, like the big boy at school, a daily advantage over the weakling; and if he could get his own way among other men, it is clear that all men, being stronger, would tend to dominate their womenfolk. The feminist, indeed, wishes us to believe that all women lived as down-trodden drudges throughout the whole of the past except during a vague period when society is supposed to have submitted, in some places, to a matriarchy. If we examine the subject of these antique matriarchies, we find that they were not at all as the feminist imagines them. We find that in certain savage tribes descent was traced through the mother because primitive people do not realise the connection between sexual intercourse and childbirth, but that nevertheless it was the men who ruled the tribe. We can say, then, that during thousands of years our world was a fighting world and that the warrior was the human ideal. Every social change, therefore, that reduced the value of muscular strength reduced also the inequality between women and men. Gunpowder, killing the strong man as easily as the weakling, counteracted nature and put an end to the Homeric or the mediæval hero. And later, when we began to settle our disputes in a law-court instead of using swords or pistols, and again when the citizen relied for safety upon a police force, women had made important gains toward an equality with men which they were not then seeking.

Similarly, the world assumed for a very long time that the bearing and rearing of children was the obvious occupation for women and that it precluded them in general from earning a livelihood by any other kind of work. The world also assumed that men should obtain the food required by themselves, their women-folk and their children, whether they did so by hunting in the forest or by toiling in the office or the workshop. For this reason the lives of women were dependent upon the labour of men, and a woman therefore became in some degree the property of the man who had undertaken to maintain her. We can understand the wrath of the feminist when she reads of a married woman who, at the end of the eighteenth century and in a rural part of England, wearing only a shift, was offered for sale as a wife to passers-by, the price for her being ten shillings; or the story, dating from 1852, of " a man who had led his wife from Burton-on-Trent, five miles away, with a halter round her neck, and then put her up for auction, parading her three times round the Cross." This woman, moreover, was bought as a wife (though the sale, of course, was illegal) for half-a-crown and half a gallon of beer. A little reflection, however, will show that the feminist's fury is in part misguided. The woman's husband was presumably no longer able to support her, and if he had not sold her to another man she would have gone into the workhouse. We ought not even to be outraged by the low price that she fetched. The purchaser—a man, no doubt, of humble station—was taking over the liability of maintaining her for an indefinite period and probably for life. As for the husband, he had sold her not so much for what he could get by the sale as for what he would save by not having to feed and clothe her.

These incidents are, of course, only extreme illustrations of the fact that men, if they are supporting women, will require some return for their labour. The poor man will value his wife as much for her work in the house as for her sexual attraction or her work as a mother. The rich man, whose wife does no work or very little, will value her chiefly as a sexual companion and as the mother of his children. He will therefore expect not work but sexual fidelity in exchange for maintenance: and this —simple as it will seem when simply stated— is the chief cause of the contention which at present rages between the sexes. It is true that until lately women accepted their inferior position partly because the Old Testament had sanctioned a patriarchal system of family life; but they also accepted a dual standard of sexual morality because any act of infidelity might involve them in social and economic disaster. Even in this matter the feminist cries out too vehemently. The man who seduced the Village Maiden was undoubtedly a scoundrel, and the lot of the seduced maiden was deplorable indeed; but the base acts of one sex have been offset by those of the other. Innumerable women, safeguarded by marriage, have led their husbands to labour in support of children who were begotten by other men; and a dispassionate judge might have to admit that the feminine crime was not the less monstrous of the two.

Except, then, on a very low level of society— the level of the slum—women are no longer at a disadvantage because they are muscularly weaker than men. In general, they are still at an economic disadvantage, and perhaps must always remain so. Their sexual disadvantage, on the other hand, has practically disappeared; and this fact has so abruptly unbalanced the relationship of the sexes that we ought to examine it at some length.

V

LÂO-TSZE, as I have reminded the reader, urged men to " account the great as little and the little as great." We have here an opportunity of applying his maxim: for although we do not realise it, we have lived through a silent and unspectacular revolution compared with which the revolutions in France and Russia were unimportant agitations. The reader will not think that I have exaggerated if he reflects that a small chemical contrivance has delivered half the women of the world from a disadvantage that is as old as civilisation itself and that, in doing so, it has altered the lives not only of half the people who are now in the world but also, we may presume, of everyone who will be born into it for thousands of years. Contraceptives, in fact, have cut us off from the past and given us a new social condition that will endure indefinitely, for the world will no more abandon the use of them than it will go back to the use of candles.

Contraceptives of a kind have, indeed, been used occasionally from distant days, but it is only in our time that they have become available to everyone. The general use and knowledge of them have annulled one of Nature's most influential laws, and if only we could get this truth into our heads we should understand why the problem of sexual morality has become so acute and so difficult to solve. A moment's meditation is enough to reveal the profound effect of contraceptives upon society, first upon the psychology and the lives of women, then— by repercussion—upon those of men.

In pre-contraceptive days, a girl risked everything—home, respect and financial support. She had to be desperately in earnest, desperately in love, before she ran that incalculable risk—or exceedingly foolish; and the man who allowed her to run it was a fool, a scoundrel, or a great lover. A girl can now satisfy her need of sexual intercourse, though not her need of motherhood, with almost complete impunity. A man, therefore, does not feel, as his father would have felt, that he is a villain if he has an affair with her; and she, in turn, can afford to enter into it without being deeply, or at all, in love. Because of this new factor there has been inevitably some cheapening of passion and a tremendous decline in romantic idealisation. There has been, too, a marked increase of companionability between the sexes. Close companionship in the old days was obviously perilous, but girls are now ready to share the responsibility and able to run the risk of letting a friend develop into a lover, and that is why the notion that a man "betrays" a girl is already obsolescent. Many girls go so far as to argue, or assume, that there is no longer any reason for behaving differently from their brothers.

Now, a young man who has experimented with Rosalind, Beatrice and Viola (lady-girls who would not have been accessible in 1900) and who afterwards wishes to marry Juliet, cannot effectively complain if Juliet has given to other men that which Rosalind, Beatrice and Viola have given to him; nor will Juliet listen contritely to a rebuke. The situation in 1900 would have been quite different. The young man might have "committed sleepery," as an American lady used to say, with one or two shop-girls at Oxford or Cambridge and have gone "home" with a prostitute now and again; but he would almost certainly never have "compromised" a lady-girl and, this being the general rule, it follows that in all probability the lady-girl (Juliet) whom he wishes to marry would still be a virgin. Because contraceptives have reduced to vanishing-point the danger of pregnancy, both Juliet and her lover have come to look upon the physical aspect of sexuality as of much less importance than either would have felt it to be before the revolution. Incidentally, the effect upon our classical literature, unless feminine free-lancing should be checked, will be startling indeed, though few people at present apprehend it; for the greater part of that literature is founded upon an assumption that women should be chaste if they wish to be respected. When the right of women to satisfy their sexual instinct is generally admitted—and the admission becomes more general with every decade— Lancelot and Guinevere may seem to be merely the martyrs of an obsolete tabu, and Othello's grief and disgust may seem, as they must already seem in Moscow, so fantastic as to lose their old appeal. Boars and sows, I believe, are untroubled by jealousy.

No sensible person can doubt that men are less lascivious than they were in the days when a woman was a foreigner. The typical young men of our time are no longer furtive. They do not hurry secretly to Paris in order to be able to look at the legs of a dancer or at the multitudinous underclothes which were exhibited by the high-kickers of the old music-halls. Indeed, we may well wonder how much longer the showmen who provide our public entertainments will calculate that an exposure of women's bodies is bound to attract the money of the public, for the new young man, accustomed to the considerable nudity of his girl-friends every August at the seaside, remains impassive before the spectacle of semi-nude strangers upon the stage or the screen. Mixing freely and at all times with young women, and even finding no difficulty in securing a friend as a temporary lover, he has become so familiar with the details of feminine life that they very soon cease to interest him, and long before he is out of his twenties he regards all women of his age very much as though they were his cousins or even his sisters.

Lasciviousness has greatly declined, then, because it can exist only when sexual interest is generally regarded as wicked. Peeping Toms were common enough in 1900. To-day most men would regard them as weaklings—much as they would regard a mere exhibitionist. For the same reason, romantic feeling between the sexes has immensely diminished, if it has not actually expired. Strangeness and diffi-culty are essential elements of romance—the glass-mountain which must be climbed, for example, the monster which must be overcome, the difficult voyage over dangerous lands or seas, the enchanted princess who can be delivered only after a long and courageous enterprise. Women, however, are no longer inaccessible, no longer strange; and the rationalist rejoices in the knock-about and unromantic attitude of young men and women toward each other. The truth is that they have reverted, as far as possible, to the sexual state of savages. The savage is promiscuous, within the rules of tabu, because he does not realise that childbirth is due to sexual intercourse. Modern young people are promiscuous, within the limits of public opinion, because they know that contraceptives will almost certainly annul the natural effects of sexual intercourse. If, though, we pause to remember the inspiration toward high art or noble action which men derived for so long from the seeming strangeness of women, we may come to think that the twentieth century has lost as much as it has gained. Nor should the triumphant rationalist too readily assume that romance was never anything but illusion and that women never were truly fit objects of idealistic devotion. He ignores the strong tendency in women to become what men desire them to be, a tendency which now causes them to suggest that they have nothing richer to give than good-fellowship. There is much truth in the wistful lines of A. E. . . .

They stilled the sweetest breath of song
    Who loosed from love its chains,
Who made it easy to be borne,
    A thing that had no pains.

A dusk has blighted Psyche's wings,
    And the wild beauty dies.
The fragrance and the glow were born
    From its own agonies.

VI

THE general use of contraceptives, then, deprived men of a substantial advantage. Women, suddenly set free from a natural inequality which had suppressed their instincts for an immense period, determined to make full use of their new liberty. Many thousands of them, intent upon demonstrating their equality in every respect with men, persuaded themselves that their sexual need was more insistent than nature had made it. Naturally chaste, many of them succeeded in thinking themselves into an unchaste life; and at the same time others, naturally over-sexed, either " took a lover with afternoon tea " (as one Society woman boasted) or openly competed for the embraces of well-known negroes.

They began in general to think more lightly —and sometimes with a flippant bravado—of virginity and of sexual " surrender." Men, finding that lady-girls were available where, in 1900, they would have had to consort with harlots or chorus-girls, performed an emotional somersault, reversed the inherited feeling of centuries and attempted, in turn, to put little value upon feminine virginity or even chastity. Within a few years they had ceased to demand either because neither could readily be found, and in this way they began to lack the fierce possessiveness of the older generation and, losing that, lost also the old passionate attachment which had made men willing to fight or even to die for their women. Marriage and divorce were no longer of great significance; nor could there any longer be much intensity in a sexual alliance which was presumably one of many and itself impermanent. By forcing men to suppress the possessiveness of the stag and the lion, women rejoiced the hearts of invertebrate sexual reformers, but they also made the emotions of men become shallow. Not only did girls expect men to marry them irrespective of any experiments in the past, but many married women affirmed their right to indulge in some measure of infidelity. The earlier male victims of this feminist movement must often have echoed the heart-cry of Shakespeare:—

> That we can call these delicate creatures ours,
> But not their appetites!

Within the last few years, however, under force of necessity, the younger men have tried to adapt themselves to a suddenly altered world and to think, feel and behave in a manner which was recommended as being " modern." At the present time, indeed, a man might as hopefully admit that he is a criminal as that he is possessive. This change is largely due to the fact that some of our socialistic reformers have spread abroad the notion that sexual possessiveness is a form of that passion for " property " which they regard as the root of all evil. They curiously associate it with capitalism, though a modest knowledge of the emotions of male animals, above a rudimentary level, should have made them realise that sexual possessiveness predates any arrangement of human society.

If we wish to account for the startling rapidity with which the sexual ideas of modern people have changed, we must appreciate one simple, fundamental and unacknowledged fact; namely, that it is impossible to overestimate the psychological need of women to be in the fashion. They themselves do not realise that their fashion instinct is stronger than their moral sense—that it is, in truth, all-pervasive. They will be sternly moral in an age of stern morality. When fashion, or the feeling of society, decreed modesty, they were excessively modest; and under the same influence they could so far forget their sexual nature as to be able without great difficulty to lead celibate lives. With the veering of fashion, however, they have complacently exposed more and more of their persons; and, caring nothing so long as numbers are on their side, they will now parade the streets of any holiday resort in costumes which none of them would have tolerated a few years ago. If fashion should so decree, they would walk naked down Broadway and would feel far less uneasy in that condition than if they were dressed but not in the mode. And if fashion should reverse its decree, making modesty once more the right aim of all up-to-date women, they would marvel that they could ever have dispensed with their clothes a few " seasons " earlier.

During the Great War they realised that to be " smart " they must be more or less promiscuous, and nothing, in consequence, could check their experiments. If we had asked a hundred women in 1920 why they were passing from man to man, a few of them would have replied that they intended to be equal in all ways with men; but the many others would have said merely that they " did not want to be ' stuffy ' "—an acknowledgment that they could no more bear to be out of the fashion sexually than in their attire.

It is surprising that women, who are rightly credited with being clear-sighted, should not perceive the final effect of their claim to sexual liberty, for that effect is both obvious and inevitable. Let us examine, then, the situation in which rationalism, strangely assisted by the popularisation of contraceptives, has placed us, and consider the new sex problems which that world-changing device has introduced. We can be quite certain that women, having learned to do most of the things which men can do, will never revert to the conditions of the Turkish harem or the Victorian home, and will never again be satisfied, even, to achieve their purposes only by their power of sexually enchanting men. Let us try also to foresee the position of women as it will be when the world has adapted itself to the startling changes of the last twenty years.

VII

WE hear far too much about the foolish young people of our time. There have always been multitudes of people, young and old, who were flippant and superficial; and although we have our full share of those who are silly, any sensitive observer must have realised that a large part of the new generation is thoughtful and serious. The young men and women of whom I am thinking find themselves in an age that has no settled morality. They find also that our sexual reformers, far from suggesting any principles which might become the nucleus of a modern morality, are contented to recommend more sexual life for everybody and to howl hysterically at the moral system of Christianity. These reformers, indeed, are delighted by the existing absence of all rules, and look forward eagerly to a state of complete moral anarchy.

Many of those who are now in the twenties, however, want much more to build up a new morality than to wallow in unrestricted licence. They recognise instinctively that anarchy is neither comfortable nor worthy of our position in the history of man. They suspect that if we can find no rules of conduct we shall be moving backwards. They are confident that, somehow or other, an instinct of self-preservation will prevent society from collapsing into mere shapelessness. At the same time, they are faced with a situation of unexampled difficulty. The majority of educated Europeans and Americans believe as little in God or the soul as the leaders of modern Russia, but only the Russians have had the intellectual energy to apply their materialism consciously and thoroughly to the management of life. The rest of us are living morally upon the capital bequeathed to us by Christianity; and everyone knows that it is impossible to live indefinitely upon capital. We have given up the religious ideas of our grandparents and are now finding that the morality which formed round those ideas is itself disintegrating— much as the shell of a snail will gradually break up when a thrush has eaten its occupant. Society, in short, is now precariously held together by an inherited morality in which people no longer believe and inevitably, decade by decade, that morality is losing its hold upon us. The late-Victorian was less ruled by biblical doctrine than were his mid-Victorian parents; the Edwardian was conspicuously lax by comparison with the late-Victorian; and the neo-Georgian, in turn, frequently startles or even distresses the ageing Edwardian. We have been using up our moral capital, and we have not found a single principle which might replace the many which we have abandoned. The situation is therefore of unexampled difficulty because, in all likelihood, no previous generation has come into the world at a time when an old moral system has so rapidly collapsed.

When we are writing or talking about sexual conduct we must always be tempted to quote from professors of biology. It is true that the habits of tadpoles or bonellia may not be a safe guide to the ideal behaviour of men and women, but we may securely suppose that human beings, in spite of their marvellous complexity, never wholly detach themselves from biological laws or tendencies. Indeed, our abilities and our social graces appear to the eyes of the biologist as mere trivial adornments, and we ourselves as links in the endless chain of life or (perhaps we could say) as magnified ova and spermatozoa.

If we want to think sanely about sex, we ought, therefore, to concentrate our thoughts upon the normal man and woman, terming them normal because they are biologically sound and, under reasonable conditions, would wish to have children and to rear them. These are the true human stock, and they are the majority of our kind. The men and women who abhor the notion of reproducing themselves are freaks who should regret their freakishness; and the inverts, who so often and so absurdly regard themselves as a chosen and superior people, ought no more to be proud of their oddity than if they were colour-blind or defective in any other way. All these minorities have, of necessity, their special problems, but for us it will be more profitable to consider the problems of the majority. We have all heard, for example, the modern quarter-truth, which imposes only upon the shallow-minded, that it is women who hunt men, not men (as the world had previously supposed) who hunt women; and the time has come when we should push this tiresome paradox into limbo. Women desire men as much as men desire women, but the sexual interest of any one man, if he is normal, crystallises round a particular woman long before she is more than generally affected by him. Very few women, in fact, initiate a love-affair. The man is the first to concentrate his attention. For a time any marriageable girl might respond equally to various men, and it is only by degrees that she consolidates her interest in one of them. Thereafter, no doubt, she instinctively proceeds to make sure of him, and it is at this point—the opening of the second act—that the paradox-monger begins to observe the drama. When, in this way, a woman psychologically enfolds a man, having first been sought out by him, the whole drama is probably a civilised version of the manner in which a male-cell, the spermatozoon, is absorbed by a female cell, the ovum.

If it were not for children there would be no sex-problem at all. Children require support for a very long time, and that is the essence of the matter: for our view of what is really about to happen, both within marriage and outside of it, must depend upon whether we believe that the majority of women will ever be able to support themselves and their children. A few—either in business or as public entertainers—can do so already: but not many people will deny that the bearing and rearing of children is likely to put most women for all time at a disadvantage as money-earners. If, then, Nature has foreordained them to look for support to the unimpeded work of men, we must outrage the sentimentalist by speaking of money and marriage in the same breath.

All modern-minded people recognise that women have sexual desires and that celibacy is often dangerous. We no longer settle the problem in the nineteenth-century manner by asserting that only evil women have any sexual hunger or that a wife, if worthy of her position, merely endures with stately acquiescence the regrettable ardours of her husband. We can see at once how far we have travelled from the nineteenth century if we remember that even Lecky, in his *History of European Morals*, confidently refers to sexual interest or desire as coming from " our lower nature." It is still more surprising to discover how deeply Winwood Reade, that ardent rationalist, remained stuck in the Victorian sentiment about sex. He tells us that cultured persons " conceive a contempt for those pleasures which they share with the lowest of mankind, and even with the brutes. They feel," he goes on, " that this instinct is degrading; they strive to resist it; they endeavour to be pure." From this he proceeds to sketch an almost evangelical picture of " the voluptuary " who " enters strange and tortuous paths which lead him to that awful borderland where all is darkness, all is horror, where vice lies close to crime "; and he adds quaintly that the voluptuary was once " as guileless as a girl " and " began by learning vice from the example of his companions, just as he learnt to smoke." What, we wonder, would this early rationalist have thought if he could have foreseen that rationalism would not only leave few girls who could rightly be termed " guileless," but would also cause innumerable men and women to regard sexual intercourse as of very little importance?

Although the prediction will horrify a Victorian and disconcert even an Edwardian, nothing could be more certain than that unmarried girls will take more and more advantage of the safeguard which contraceptives provide. Some girls may prefer to keep their virginity until they marry, but the virginal wife-caste of 1900 will completely disappear. Young men, in consequence, will have to crush out their innate possessiveness, at least before marriage, and for some time society will cease to set a high value upon feminine virginity. By forcing men to modify their natural feelings, women will do away with the age-long distinction between the honoured woman and the woman who is mainly a sexual toy. The young of both sexes will associate upon that equality which the feminist so vehemently advocates, and the men, necessarily, will take for granted that they have no more responsibility than the girls. Sexual intercourse, becoming a commonplace of youthful life, will no longer form the peak of emotional experience, as it did for most men until lately, but will be an alternative to other amusements —to a game of lawn-tennis or a half-hour in a speed-boat. There will be much good-fellowship between the sexes, but none of that poetic emotion which is embalmed in *Romeo and Juliet* or *La Vita Nuova*, nor will " love " be sufficiently complex to form the central interest of novels and plays. People, in fact, will no longer think of love and sexual attraction as being one and the same thing; and just as there is now a faded and old-world feeling in the words " a Valentine," so will there be a similar feeling in 1950 associated with the words " a love-affair." A young man's interest in young women already becomes languid at an early age. Most men in 1950 will not regard any girl as worth fighting for, just as nobody now would go to the stake for his religious creed. In short, the New Man will emerge, as the New Woman emerged in 1890. He will be unpossessive and unidealistic : and so will he continue until the tone of society changes under the influence of a masculine counter-offensive which few people apparently at present foresee.

Even during the transition period, which began about twenty years ago and may persist for another twenty years, the cry for sexual freedom and the same standard of conduct for both sexes will not lead to complete promiscuity. Instinct will continue to upset the arrangements of reason. Most women will find that, no matter how " sensible " it might be and no matter how greatly they wish to be equal with men, they still cannot bring themselves to be the first to woo; most men will find, to their shame, that they cannot entirely cease to feel possessively; both men and women will discover that a sexual association does form an irrationally close bond; and sometimes, in spite of the scientific atmosphere about them, an instinct toward personal devotion will intensify an affair which they had intended to be casual. Prudery, however, will no more return than the sedan-chair or the nose-ring; and that will be one of the triumphs of the twentieth century.

VIII

IN many primitive societies there is one standard of conduct for the unmarried and another for the married, very much more freedom being permitted to the former. Posterity, in all probability, will make a similar distinction. Feminists and reformers at present, however, do not stop short at the claim that a modern girl ought, before marriage, to be as free as her brother to make sexual experiments and so to gain valuable experience. They hope for a halcyon age in which, for example, a husband, if he has been unfaithful, will cheerfully recognise the right of his wife to follow suit. They affirm, with strange confidence, that there is no disparity between the sexual needs of men and those of women, and that now, in an age of contraceptives, there is no ground for demanding that a wife should live more strictly than her husband. At first sight a dual standard—one law for the man and another for the woman—appears to be obviously unjust; and it is here that women have stolen a march upon the slower-witted sex.

Nothing could be more unjust than the establishment of a single moral standard for husbands and wives alike.

Upon most levels of life a man is able to secure a housekeeper for much less than it costs him to maintain a wife. In these days, too,—thanks to the sexual crusade of the feminist—he can find a lover without looking very far afield. His purpose in marrying, therefore, is to have children of his own begetting and a companion who shall assuage his innate sexual possessiveness. If his wife claims and exercises a right to take lovers, his assurance of paternity will be gone. Contraceptives, far from bettering his position, add much to its danger. They encourage a wife, if she is so inclined, to experiment. No contraceptive is entirely reliable, but, with marriage to uphold her, a woman might run the risk of pregnancy with little or no misgiving. If she were anxious to have no more children, legitimate or illegitimate, she would doubtless take every possible precaution; but either through carelessness or excitement, or even on purpose, many women would become pregnant by their lovers, and only one in a million would resist the overwhelming temptation to secure the child's position and life-long support by attributing it to the husband.

Here, then, we see that if sexual equality in

marriage should prevail, men will occupy an absurd position. A man may do many social injuries to his wife, but nothing which he can do, short of a permanent physical injury, could compare with the villainy of a wife who causes her husband to work for twenty years or longer in order to support a child whom he wrongly supposes to be his own. We can realise the severity of the punishment which ought to be visited upon the woman who so deceives a man, if we imagine what punishment we should demand were one man unjustly to enslave another for the best years of his life. And even if anyone should declare that contraceptives have reduced to a minimum the risk of illegitimate pregnancy, he would not have disposed of the economic factor in marriage. A man cannot fairly be expected to support his wife in order that she may give sexual pleasure to another man. He cannot fairly be expected to labour at his office or elsewhere in order that she may be able, for example, to buy new clothes for the express purpose of delighting her paramour and of strengthening her hold on his interest. The husband, in this situation, is supporting himself, his wife and the paramour of some other man. The perfervid feminist would indignantly assert that by taking this view of the subject we are treating a woman as though she were the property of a man. The answer is easy—that no wealthy woman married to a poor man would finance him for the gratification of a rival; and that which nobody would demand of a woman ought obviously not to be demanded of a man.

When we say that a woman should be sexually faithful to her husband (unless, of course, they have agreed to go their own ways), we are not saying that she is his property, but that she ought to keep to her half of the bargain. Although charm and sentiment gracefully smothered it, like a creeper on a brick wall, the pre-feminist marriage was a bargain in which the man offered lifelong maintenance and the woman lifelong fidelity. The husband, in fact, was paying for the possession of a chaste woman. I do not mean that he had no other interest in his wife, but that, no matter what graces and abilities she might possess, he would not have wanted her if she had not guaranteed her fidelity. Right up to the present day a man has married for two purposes: the first, to have children and to feel assured that he fathers none but his own children, and the second, that he might enjoy that sexual possessiveness which he shares with most male animals. To-day, however, we are told that he must outgrow his possessiveness and, if required to do so, permit his wife to have sexual intercourse with other men This modern cant about the criminality of male possessiveness will persist until men wake up to the lopsidedness of a modernistic marriage. No man is so sexually happy as when he feels barbarically possessive, and it may be that most women are happiest when they feel that they are the possession of a man whom they love and respect. To rebuke men for their animal possessiveness is like rebuking them because they have to shave their chins. Again, we cannot scotch the possessiveness of the male without rendering him careless and tepid in his sex relationships. Nobody treasures a library-book, and no man will care passionately for a woman who in a week's time may be in the arms of some other man. The reformers assure us that we must no longer regard the sexual aspect of marriage as the most important, or even as being important at all; but if we do as they bid we are making marriage hardly distinguishable from a friendship between persons of opposite sex, but with the fantastic difference that the man is to pay —in other words, to work hard—for the sake of maintaining a woman-friend.

It is indeed strange that so few men and so few women can see how contraceptives and the modern attitude toward sexuality have affected the marriage-partnership. Men, still bemused by the sentiment which civilisation has woven into marriage, continue to make themselves liable for the lifelong support of women who offer no more than a temporary "mistress" can offer. The blindness of women, however, is even more astonishing. By claiming the right to as much sexual liberty as men, they themselves are providing men with sexual companions who render marriage not so necessary and not so attractive; and when they proceed to expect men to marry them, they are looking for a type of man who will be fantastically content to pay for a wife and to receive only what a friend or a housekeeper could give in exchange. In this way the sexual emancipation of women threatens to take away from them their very livelihood; and the sexual victory of the feminist will turn into the economic rout of women. At present they do not realise what they have done because most men still marry in a Victorian mood. As the years pass, however, men will realise in larger and larger numbers that marriage without fidelity on the part of the woman is a ludicrous one-sided partnership, and fewer and fewer men will be prepared to burden themselves with a lifelong liability. Women, in fact, if they do not wish to destroy marriage, and by so doing to face the necessity of supporting themselves, will have to make it more attractive than the free love which they themselves now advocate. They can do so only by giving men the two-fold assurance which men need—that their wives will not be the paramours of other men, and that their wives' children will be of their own begetting.

We shall see, therefore, a great decline in marriage, and the wiseacres will scratch their heads in an effort to account for it. This will form the masculine counter-offensive—an unreasoned boycott of marriage; and when the situation has become acute, women—most of whom would always rather have children and security than outside work and independence—will unconsciously adapt themselves to the new situation. They will regard the free-loving women as blacklegs, who are acting against the interests of women in general; the vogue of the chaste woman will return; the plausible theory that men and women should have equal sexual freedom will become (even perhaps in the United States) a curious episode in social life. When we hear, as a well-known London magistrate observed a few months ago, that over and over again working-class women will marry, goad their husbands into violence or desertion, and then apply to the Courts for separation and maintenance—the whole drama having been premeditated from the first—we may well wonder how long the working-class man will put his head into the noose. In pre-feministic days natural sexuality forced men—or most men—to marry. At the present time, women, by their very insistence upon sexual freedom, are rendering marriage unnecessary.

IX

THE reader, I am sure, must feel that I have exaggerated the situation as it now is or as it soon may be, and must have suspected that the "immorality" of certain "advanced" groups has misled me into fancying that all modern men and women are unfaithful and unscrupulous; but he should remember that traditional morality is bound to grow steadily weaker as the Victorians and Edwardians gradually die out. The people of the near future will have an exceedingly difficult problem to solve. They will admit that women ought not to be sexually starved; but they will also admit that a wife ought not to expect that her husband shall finance her infidelities; and in looking for a solution, they will not be able to appeal to the patriarchal morality of the Bible. Unmarried girls and all self-supporting women will undoubtedly follow their own inclinations; and public feeling is likely to change so much that when self-supporting women have children without being married, "the world" will think no worse of their behaviour than it now thinks of divorce. And after several generations, the Law—that giant sloth —will adjust itself to the common practice of society.

For some years women will continue to claim the right to take lovers if a marriage goes wrong; and indeed, having admitted that neither women nor men should sexually starve, we may well wonder what a woman ought to do when her husband has lost all sexual interest in her. At present she is supposed to resign herself to lifelong celibacy; but for how many more years will public opinion condemn a woman of, say, twenty-five to such a difficult, nerve-straining and even perilous lot? For sometimes—as when there is a child of the marriage—the husband and wife may feel that they must live together even if they can no longer find sexual happiness in one another. A grim burden, in such a case, is bound to fall upon either the man or the woman: the man having to support his wife while she is the paramour of another, or the woman having to go without sexual stimulus because she is dependent upon her husband. A man, clearly, ought not to be able to abandon his wife when he tires of her, nor will he ever be allowed to do so, but neither ought a woman to be able to find sexual satisfaction elsewhere so long as she is dependent upon her husband; and the least unfair solution of this problem would be for the woman to make herself as economically independent as possible by finding remunerative work. For the reasons already given, a dual standard of sexual morality in marriage is likely, in general practice, to return.

No sensible person will construe this hard saying into a plea for male promiscuity. Neither women nor men who have any kindness of heart will wantonly hurt the feelings or injure the legitimate self-respect of a marriage-partner. Nevertheless, if we are not fanatics we must admit that a man's infidelity, apart from current tradition, is not so disruptive as a woman's. It is also, biologically, more pardonable. It is not so disruptive because—once more—a man cannot, as Dr. Johnson observed, "introduce confusion of progeny"—in other words, cannot deceive his wife by pretending that his extra-marital children are also hers. It is more pardonable because a man's part in sexual intercourse is over within a few minutes, while those few minutes are meant by Nature to involve a woman in changes that cover perhaps a year. By nature, therefore, a man is very soon free to enter again into sexual intercourse, and in an unfettered society would, Pan-like, pursue a second nymph. Only if we believe that human beings have completely outgrown their biological beginnings can we maintain tha men have not more difficulty than womer in remaining monogamous. Over-civilisation may make women over-sexual, but Nature has arranged the matter so inequitably that for a woman sexual fulfilment requires as many months as it requires minutes for a man.

The future will have no moral code. In place of a moral code, sanctioned by religious ideas, it will have a code of honour and of good taste. Men, on account of contraceptives, will have to rely more and more upon the good faith of their wives, and for this reason they will unconsciously choose for marriage the women who give the most promise of honesty. The wife who imposes her illegitimate child upon her husband will be looked upon as a criminal, a criminal of baser kind than any mere blackmailer. Ultimately, however, sexual behaviour will be assessed in the balance of good taste. At present there is a shallow-minded reaction against the pronouncements of psycho-analysis, but when this reaction is over we shall recognise that there is very little in either a man or a woman that has not a sexual basis. People will become more and more biologically-minded, will see themselves more and more as good or bad transmitters of life and, in that awareness, will realise that to live unhealthily is a crime against the future.

Even now there are signs that health will be the cult of the future. And not less important will be their realisation that no human being can give " the body " alone. Just because our complicated personalities are so deeply rooted in sex, we give a large part of ourselves when we share our sexuality with another. A woman will regard herself, for example, as either a glass of rare wine or a mug of porter; and the woman who is casual and promiscuous in her sex-affairs will be regarded as one who has a very low opinion of herself and of what she is giving. A woman, in fact, who has any self-respect will less easily share her body with a man whom she does not richly love than she would share her dresses and her underclothing with mere acquaintances. Women, moreover, when they find that men, no longer hazed by sentiment, are turning away from marriage, will instinctively encourage that very possessiveness of the male which many of them are now attempting to extirpate, and this they will only be able to do by living chastely and so making themselves valuable. As for men, they have always held together in a greater degree than women, and even now the man who consorts carnally with the wife of another man, unless her marriage has completely broken down, is seldom at ease in his mind. When good taste has the social power of a moral code a man will no more think of appropriating another man's wife or mistress than he would think of using another man's house or car, or, let us say, even his umbrella.

We despise a glutton. We certainly do not admire a drunkard. We realise that in eating and drinking self-discipline and balance are obviously desirable. In the future, people will acknowledge that sexual promiscuity, far from being a gallant crusade against inhibitions, is a vulgar misuse of personality. On the one hand, they will not submit to the rigid morality of the nineteenth century; on the other, they will despise promiscuity as blunting the edge of a delicate delight, and will class the man or woman who is sexually promiscuous with the man or woman who drinks wine solely in order to stupefy the senses and the mind.

X

THE two subjects which have occupied us for so long begin at this point to converge. Religion and sex are the strongest of our interests, unless indeed we consider that for many people the lure of money or fame or power is a third and equal competitor. This being so, it is not at all surprising that religion has very often made bitter war upon sexual instinct, or that those of our would-be reformers who are sex-obsessed should make war just as bitterly upon religion. These persons can never refer to religion, and in particular to Christianity, without abusing it, and the reason is, of course, that Christianity and many other religions have unquestionably crusaded vehemently against " sex."

It was not so always. Long ago, primitive people, feeling that life and its transmission were exceedingly mysterious, adored graven images of the sexual organs. Having no economic difficulties and being still closely in touch with biological purpose, they worshipped fertility and praised it with ecstatic

dances and hymns. To them nothing whatever seemed more marvellous than sex; and
under the disguises of civilisation there are
many persons even now who would like to
exalt sexual union into a religious experience.
The two great impulses were still blended
in the so-called religious prostitution of girls
in Chaldæa and in parts of India. We all
know, too, how grievously certain pieces of
Indian sculpture have shocked our sex-
denouncing missionaries. Even Mahommed,
founding one of the world's great religions,
did not consider sexuality to be its enemy.
That religion and sex are enemies, however,
was definitely the view of Buddhism, Pytha-
goreanism, Christianity, Neo-Platonism and
many other religions or philosophies, and this
is the view which has prevailed in most parts
of the world for an immense number of years.
The results have sometimes been lamentable
indeed. For three centuries, if not for a
much longer period, very few men and women
have felt cleanly about sex; and no one would
assert that everybody, even now, has outgrown the notion that there is something
shameful in it. If we were as clear-minded
about sexuality as we claim to be, half the jokes
that amuse us would be pointless and un-
marketable.

The modern sceptic, desiring to see the whole

matter with fresh and scientific eyes, often declares, without more palaver, that all religious preoccupation is morbid or superstitious and that religion opposes sex only because its devotees have unwholesome minds. So shallow a diagnosis of that old opposition is not likely to satisfy any careful thinker. He will probably decide, rather, that there must have been a deep and powerful cause for the rebellion against sexual instinct which appears so early in our history. Perhaps he will judge that religion decried sex because it recognised in sex the most formidable of its rivals, and that if kleptomania had been as universal and as persistent as sexual desire, religion would have concentrated its attack upon kleptomania. A man has only a limited amount of psychic energy at his disposal, and it is obvious that if he spends it in one way he will have less of it to spend in another. Again, every religion and every moral system is an attempt to discipline human nature: and if we are to have any self-discipline at all, it is clear that the strongest of our instincts will require the strongest control.

Unfortunately, though, once a man has recognised that within himself there is a civil warfare between what he is by nature and what he feels that he ought to be—in a word, between his body and his soul—he is greatly tempted to cultivate his "higher" self with a fanatical intensity. That is precisely what happened to all those men and women of the past who practised an extreme asceticism. Many of them became more interested in suppressing their life-instincts than in developing their love-impulses. Hundreds—it may be, thousands—of persons have wasted their time, their energy, the whole of their lives, by concentrating upon the suppression of their natural instincts. A few moments of loving action toward their fellow-creatures would have done more for humanity—and more for their own souls—than all those years of negative effort; and many a man who was no Galahad may have been more spiritually effective than the mere self-mortifying saint. We may think that the puritan's hatred of sexuality is absurd, exaggerated and often unclean, but in its origin it is noble. Men turn against sex when they believe themselves to have found a less primitive use for vitality and intelligence; but, although it is difficult enough to tame wild instinct, it is immeasurably more difficult to expand beyond ourselves. The puritan, having set out with the intention of spiritualising himself, forgets his course and ends up by destroying that which he thinks to be evil, rather than by developing that which he once knew to be good.

To-day, having no religion—neither one that is beautiful because it comes from love nor one that is unwholesome because it comes from a negation of instinct—we do not think of sexuality as being either horrible or holy. We believe that the sensible man will allow the life-instincts within him a fair measure of fulfilment, and that if he does not spend the greater part of his energy in crushing them out, he will actually be freer to develop the mental or the spiritual part of his being. Most people agree that there is something distorted and ludicrous about the man or woman who can be interested in nothing but sex. Our basis may be biological, but to live solely as a biological specimen would seem retrograde to anyone who can appreciate the vast super-structure of civilised interests. A wise man said once: " We are souls as well as tax-payers," and in like manner we can say that a man should do more with his lifetime than merely to transmit his life. We ought, for example, to make that life worth inheriting, and this we can do only by striving hard to build up a just, beautiful and kindly world. Even the Russian materialists exhort their young people " not to waste their time and energy upon sex," the better alternative being, presumably, increased output in the factory. We can at least say that, while not denying sex, as the puritan denies it, we ought to use it in a manner that is becoming to mental creatures. The rationally-minded often ask us to admire the French view of sex (or what they take to be that view), on the ground that the French are sensible enough to separate " sex " from their other interests. The Nordics, however, mingling sex with mind and aspiration, may well have progressed to a further milestone in the journey of man. Above all, the whole subject will look somewhat differently if we believe that we are spiritual beings, not to be snuffed out by death, and it may be of interest to consider religion and sex from the point of view which the earlier part of this book attempted to describe.

XI

IF it is true that there is in man an immortal
element—one that has the utmost difficulty
in making itself felt because the life in him is
so passionate—we shall see that when religion
declares war upon sexual instinct we are
watching a struggle between the soul and the
life in a man. Their battle-ground is, perhaps,
the brain; and it may even be true that the
brain was developed so arduously for the
express purpose of giving the two combatants
within us a practicable jousting-field. From
this angle we can see that religion may so often
have opposed sex not only because it recognised
in sex the most powerful of its rivals, but also
for a deeper reason. The Hindu sages may
have been right when they announced that
sexual force could be converted into spiritual
" illumination " (" The Fire of Kundalini ");
and it may have been a vague apprehension
of this possibility which caused men so long
ago to turn against the instinct of the life
within them. The confident rationalist would
smile at a suggestion that pre-Darwinian men,

and they dark-skinned, may have known more about the mystery of sex than all the professors in Europe and the United States. Time will adjudicate between the ancients and the moderns; and it is at least possible that future professors will pity the narrow knowledge of the wise men who now instruct us.

Even if we believe that sexual instinct is a manifestation of life and has, primarily, no connection with the life-enveloped soul, we should not imitate the puritan and become fanatically antisexual. On the contrary, we ought to perceive that if sex has done much to cloud man's consciousness of himself as a spiritual being, it has sometimes done much to aid the slow self-revelation of the soul. The soul, like a suffused light, touches, however faintly, every part of intelligence with which it is associated, and that which begins in lust may end in love. Sexual desire, indeed, may have done more than anything else, in the earlier phases of human history, to develop tenderness and sympathy, and so—in some natures—it may do still.

There are, of course, twenty thousand attitudes of mind toward sex, but in general we are now in much more danger of under-valuing it than of over-exalting it. Danger lies, for example, in the characteristic view of our time—that since the soul was a mere illusion, sex is wholly animal, and that if it is wholly animal it is of no great significance, one of various physical functions which are hardly worthy to be mixed up with the mind. There is danger also in what we may call the astronomical view. To have seen the world, in imagination, from the Milky Way, is to suppose that our troubles and our triumphs are infantile; and some people, remembering the brevity and the littleness of all human affairs, come to feel that sexual problems are microscopically trivial. If we say, however, that an act of adultery on the part of two human beings is of no more importance than if it had been committed by a pair of ants, we ought to maintain that war, cruelty, injustice and starvation are of no account. We ought, in fact, to sit down and die. To take up this attitude is to see life out of focus, and that, in turn, is not to see it at all. We are then attempting to exist as though we were gods, not men; for the earth is our temporary home, and it is the earth which must give us our scale of measurement so long as we are living upon it. We have not the outfit which enables us to live and think on the scale of enormous beings who might feel themselves to be at home among the wildernesses of the Milky Way.

This, then, is a danger that comes from judging ourselves merely by our physical size.

There is just as much danger in trying prematurely to live as though we were already disembodied. The man who attempts to live as though he were a pure spirit, though rare enough to be admirable, is likely to share the fate of Icarus, for if he had a right to purely spiritual existence he would probably not have found himself in this world. Moreover, as he would learn to his sorrow, he would have as much difficulty in being of use to other men as if he could speak only a language peculiar to himself. In a word, he would be an unintelligible foreigner.

The best type of man, if he recognises that he is a spiritual being, will also recognise that he has a mortal personality, and when he sets himself to adjust the relationship of the two he will not hesitate, having some common sense, to prefer the interests of that part in him which will survive death. At the same time, he will not mortify or despise the temporary part of which his sexuality is so powerful a factor. He ought to be able to distinguish between the promptings of the immortal essence within him and the desires of that vitality which he has inherited from millions of ancestors. Here —in his sexual nature—is a marvellous legacy, handed down from the unimaginable time when life first pulsed in this world; something, in short, that merits respect, something which is no less remarkable because it is common to all sentient creatures. Many a time I have heard women belittle child-bearing, and complain that it is a process which they share with animals and even insects; but if the soul is a reality, there is much difference between the automatic and the considered reproduction of life. The best type of man, therefore, will accept his natural destiny and beget children, but he will do so without losing sight of his spiritual aims. He will certainly realise that generations of unwholesome repression have made many people think of " sex " in a filthy manner, but he himself will see it as something which is as harmless and as blameless as the budding of a bough or the up-springing of corn. Wherever he sees that cunning intelligence has debased it, he will do his best to bring the debaser into contempt, as when, for example, a cinema manager or the foreman in a factory, abusing his power and mixing two sections of life which have no natural connection, offers work to a girl in exchange for the sexual use of her body; for to persuade a girl to use her sexuality without feeling affection when she does so, is to make her act as though she were not partly a spiritual being. It is a two-fold blasphemy, a misuse alike of the soul and of sexual instinct. Nevertheless, he will look with a kindly eye upon the lovers who make dalliance in parks or lanes or shadowy byways, even although the lovers may be uncomely and the dalliance elephantine, seeing in all such expression nothing foul or reprehensible, but only a feeble and degenerate version of those hymns and dances in honour of Demeter or Aphrodite which once were executed with grace or grandeur. And of his own part in that ancient rite, he will acknowledge that he should use his sexual instinct for the purpose of life itself—for the begetting of healthy children—but also, seeing that he has an excess of it, for deepening his relationship with someone whom he loves.

Such a man, moreover, bearing in mind that death will descend upon him before many years have been added to history, will realise that he must then become a being to whom sexual interest or the pleasures of power, wealth or fame shall seem as remote as the amusements of small children seem to a man of seventy; but so long as he is alive he will play hard at life, as though it were a strenuous game, and yet all the time will so far detach himself from sensual or egotistical preoccupations that death may disembody and finally depersonalise him without an agony of rending.

XII

LET the puritan think as he must—it was not sex that brought sin into the world and all our woe. Sex has probably given humanity delight and anguish in equal measure, and if we cry it down we must rank ourselves with those pessimists who hate the earth, wish they had never been born and believe that life is both loathsome and without purpose.

All the ills of humanity, however, are due (or in the judgment of one earth-dweller seem unquestionably to be due) to a single cause, and the name of that cause is egoism. If we could cure that, we should find that we had cured all lesser evils, except physical maladies, and the great sexual instinct itself would be powerless to do harm, and become only an accessory of love, a source of heart-easing delight. So long, on the contrary, as men and women continue to be atoms of raging egoism, we shall continue to live in a state of discord and injustice. The jealousy of the artist, the knavery of the business man, the self-importance of the society woman, the brutality of the gangster and even the bad manners of insensitive persons, all arise from the violent egoism which is innate in everything that is life-possessed, from our strong sense of our own reality and our inability to absorb the fact that everyone else is no less real. The greater part of written history, too, with its memories of cruelty, aggression, craftiness and international contention, is nothing but a chronicle of fierce egoisms. The very conception of an ego, said Buddha, is the great heresy which prevents men from seeing the truth about themselves; and although humanity will never grasp the difficult doctrine that the ego is an illusion, we have some reason for hoping that men will gradually outgrow the extreme self-absorption of childhood. The unwritten history of our race is more creditable than its written record, and as the centuries have passed painfully across the world we have been slowly developing more goodwill and more fellow-feeling. Even communism exhorts men to think less of their own than of the general welfare; and even aeroplanes and wireless inevitably force upon us a rudimentary sense of world kinship. No political, economic or mechanical changes, however, can dig up the roots of our trouble. Egoism, which comes from the life principle, can only be cured by love, which comes from the life-transcending soul; and the true purpose of religion, therefore, is to make war not upon sexual instinct, but upon the egoism of life itself.

In practice the subjugation of egoism is a peculiarly difficult task. Not only are we attempting, with midget strength, to reverse the gigantic engine of nature, but, if we shed our egoism in an egoistic world, we run the danger of becoming merely meek and mild, merely soft and ineffectual. A man does well to work hard for any kind of power so long as he remembers that in the huge pageantry of time he is of exceedingly small account and that power, when achieved, should be used for the benefit of as many other persons as possible. We do not help humanity by allowing the egomaniac to push us, or anyone else, to the wall, and there is no virtue in submitting to wrongs which we should resent if they were imposed upon another. To do as we would be done by is truly a golden rule; but we might add a second, and say that we should not let others do to us what we would not do to them.

EPILOGUE

READERS who belong to certain mental types—those, in particular, who pride themselves upon their practical tendency and those who pride themselves upon their intellectual ingenuity—might say, if they had read this book, that I have done nothing more than to suggest, as many hundreds of amiable writers and public men have suggested, that what the world needs is a greater measure of love. They would be right. Indeed, I do not believe that there is any other cure for the world's ills than that which was presented with such beauty and simplicity by the most influential of all mystics, the great teacher who was born at Nazareth. And yet, in my own defence, I would state clearly that I do not suppose that the Kingdom of Love is at hand. On the contrary, as any sympathetic companion whom I have had while he read these pages will discern, I believe that the history of mankind, if it is seen spiritually, if it is seen as perhaps we shall see it very plainly when we have died, is the history of an exceedingly slow and painful emergence of love through a heavy atmosphere of lust, ambition, fear, envy and all the dark emanations of egoism. The emergence of love will be very gradual indeed, but the full emergence of love, the full revelation of the immortal self within this world of mortality is, in my view, the climax to which humanity, and perhaps all sentient creatures, are imperceptibly progressing. And in the sphere of practical behaviour—in the matter of what we should do, what we should refrain from doing and, in short, of how we should live—I would say that actions which make for union and harmony are good, and those that make for separation and discord are bad. Again, I would say that self-spiritualisation is not to be achieved by any negative practices: not to be achieved by refraining from this or from that, but only by acting, thinking and feeling disinterestedly, as though we did truly apprehend that every other creature is a centre of emotion as vivid as our own.

At the present time there is a desolation of heart among all the young people who are too thoughtful or too sensitive to be drugged or satisfied by superficial excitements. I know, from experience, that time and again more than a few of them think secretly of suicide;

and the man who smiles at this statement is a man who does not see what is happening around him. Thirty amusements or external distractions now exist and call to the younger generation where, in 1900, there was only one. The result, strangely ignored by our public men, is that concentration of interest or purpose is so difficult as to be almost impossible for those who are now in the twenties. They must always be opening their minds to some fresh external stimulus—a drive in a car, a visit to the picture-house, a dash to a night-club or some other of the many diversions which modern life provides. We cannot be surprised if they lack singleness of purpose, if they have no inner life, if they are restless and ineffectual, if they cannot content themselves with work of which the fruits are certain to come slowly. They are victims of the great mechanical age. And because modern life calls them to amuse themselves in a hundred ways, they soon find that the roots of their being are drying up. The contemplation which art requires, the meditation which religion requires, are strangled within them by the dense and poisonous overgrowth of objective interests. They alone can save themselves; and they can save themselves from spiritual atrophy only by resolutely refusing, as Odysseus refused, to be side-tracked by the syrens. If they do not, the trade, the art and the literature of our century will inevitably become invertebrate and feeble. Concentration was never more difficult to practise than it is now, but concentration and firm self-discipline alone can enable us to give our century a rich and powerful character; nor will the new generation derive any assistance in character-building from most of our eminent writers, for these writers, however confident their tone, are merely expositors of their age and persons who stimulate the fever which is everywhere about us.

One of the most conspicuous results of modern conditions is the inability of the new generation to take delight in simple and costless beauty. A day may be worth living if we see, and appreciate, the silhouette of a row of chimney-pots against the pale gold clouds of evening. A patch of blue sky should make us happier than any Hollywood film; and it fails to do so because we have no eyes or ears for anything that is not mechanical and sophisticated. The young men and women of whom I am thinking are worthy of much sympathy. The discontinuous conditions of modern life make them restless: their restlessness, in turn, prevents them from effectively standing out against those conditions: and in this way, they are jazzed from bad to worse. They want instant results from their work as they want instant excitement from their recreations—the quickly-changing, mind-scattering effects of the cinema, for example, rather than the massive up-building of a great book or drama. If they are so fortunate as to have work to do, they lack the stamina to continue doing it year after year. If they have no work to do, they degenerate morally and mentally as unused muscle will degenerate. And finding no work to their hands or no zest for it when it comes, they feel that the world has no use for them and that human life is aimless. Some, indeed, assuming that they are mere " mortal creatures of a thousand days," can see no reason for working or for building up character, a process never un-accompanied by the spiritual pain of self-discipline and mortification of the ego. Nor is it at all surprising that at last many of them, distracted by modernity, made will-less by the breakdown of religion and morality, and thwarted by the bitter economic state of the immediate present, do come to feel that the only alternatives are death or a frantic pursuit of shallow and unnourishing amusements.

In time this diagnosis will seem incredible: for in time the spiritual world, ever fretting against the envelope of the palpable world around us, will have glowed through it with sufficient strength to change the thought-tone of all serious people, and the influence upon society of one strong-charactered person counteracts the foolishness of a hundred drifters. In time a new attitude of mind, resolute and serious, will emerge, but it is not likely to supersede the contemporary use or misuse of life for many a year.

Meanwhile, what we want is a determination to see life nobly, to take it seriously, to use it worthily; and this we shall not achieve so long as we allow sensation to drown thought, so long as we tamely submit the moulding of our minds to writers who are merely cynical, negative, destructive and palsied by a little understanding of science, so long as we believe that thought without the wings of intuition can bring us to the truth about ourselves and our destiny, or so long as we take for granted that there is no world but the physical world, and will not even trouble to consider whether that physical world may be nothing more than a pageant of effects which have their causes elsewhere on the further side of death. When men and women have recovered from the violent fever induced by the sudden influx of scientific knowledge, and recapture a realisation that while they live they are mere shadows and brain-bound fragments of what they are in essence, then they will perceive that half the dissensions which divide them are not worth wrangling over, that there is a purpose in aiming at moral strength and beauty, even in relation to sex, that sexual behaviour is of deep import, and that humanity may, after all, be the spiritual centre of the universe, a diamond in a surrounding mass of slag.